The
Enneagram
in
Marriage

The Enneagram in Marriage

Your Guide to
Thriving Together
in Your Unique Pairing

Christa Hardin

BakerBooks

a division of Baker Publishing Group
Grand Rapids, Michigan

© 2023 by Christa Hardin

Published by Baker Books
a division of Baker Publishing Group
Grand Rapids, Michigan
www.bakerbooks.com

Printed in the United States of America

Library of Congress Cataloging-in-Publication Data
Names: Hardin, Christa, 1979– author.
Title: The enneagram in marriage : your guide to thriving together in your unique pairing / Christa Hardin.
Description: Grand Rapids : Baker Books, a division of Baker Publishing Group, [2023] | Includes bibliographical references.
Identifiers: LCCN 2022051806 | ISBN 9781540903372 (paperback) | ISBN 9781540903600 (casebound) | ISBN 9781493443239 (ebook)
Subjects: LCSH: Marriage—Psychological aspects. | Interpersonal relations.
Classification: LCC HQ734 .H266 2023 | DDC 306.81—dc23/eng/20230111
LC record available at https://lccn.loc.gov/2022051806

Scripture quotations are from THE HOLY BIBLE, NEW INTERNATIONAL VERSION®, NIV® Copyright © 1973, 1978, 1984, 2011 by Biblica, Inc.® Used by permission. All rights reserved worldwide.

The author is represented by the literary agency of The Christopher Ferebee Agency, www.christopherferebee.com.

The names and details of the people and situations described in this book have been changed or presented in composite form in order to ensure the privacy of those with whom the author has worked.

Baker Publishing Group publications use paper produced from sustainable forestry practices and post-consumer waste whenever possible.

23 24 25 26 27 28 29   7 6 5 4 3 2 1

This is dedicated to the brave souls out there
who faithfully rise each day to share
their beautiful gifts amid the shadows.
Your courage is my muse, and it is my honor
to walk alongside you here.

CONTENTS

Introduction

It is better to enlighten than merely to shine.

THOMAS AQUINAS[1]

Every couple's love story has the potential to brighten the world. This includes the two of you and your love story, even if your relationship doesn't feel all that dynamic these days. The truth is, your individual gifts have the potential to combine with one another, casting a beautiful and unique light into a world of shadows. Together you have a distinctive form. You bring your shared wisdom, your creativity, and a unique love to the world that no one else can offer in exactly the same way.

Along with your light, however, you can also cast shadows together in the world, creating disappointment and sometimes great big messes for one another and for future generations to clean up. If you've been in a relationship or family for any given amount of time, you know this well. You've likely experienced the interplay of lights and shadows cast from generations before you.

None of us are perfect, and even with the best of intentions, things fall apart. We've all intentionally or unintentionally shaped or influenced generations coming up alongside or under us.

In my marriage, for instance, my husband and I love shining into the world together by providing family and friends with special bonding experiences. We've put on couples events in large ballrooms, we've written and hosted mystery dinner game parties together, and we've taken most of our twenty nieces and nephews on various adventures, not to mention our own three kids. This is all on top of our jobs as helpers in medicine and mental health, where our dreams span even broader.

At our best, our combined personality gifts have taught us that with hard work and big dreams, many times there are rewards at the end of each checkpoint on the trails of life. I'm sure you have similar stories of climbing metaphorical or even real-life peaks together as you bring shared dreams to life.

As my husband and I bring what we hope are joyful experiences to others, if we're not careful to find rest and balance, our lights can burn out. As a couple, we can miss the heartbeat of one another or our kids in our zeal to help so many others.

When we're flying high, it's sunshine and good vibes all day. However, in darker moments of life, our unhealthy patterns tend to rise up in defense. Then all the adventuring in the world, no matter how glorious the peaks, can't save us from shadows and sorrows.

One such memory that reminds me of this truth is a family hike we did up Beehive Mountain in beautiful Acadia National Park. Our family of five was just finishing a vacation in Maine, the beautiful home state of my late mother. My father had also recently passed away, so I wanted to visit their special old haunts, such as the Boston train station where they had their first stolen glances and the house where my mother grew up.

My family and I were completely taken in by the slower pace of the coastal lifestyle. We ate New England clam chowder, visited historic sites, and stuffed ourselves with "lobstah" rolls. We were highly committed to experiencing a different ice cream shop every night on the dazzling harbor-front downtown. It was great!

However, as the trip wound down, I started to feel a bit uncomfortable. The losses started to really hit into my vacation mode. I laughed a bit harder to make up for it. I read books, watched funny shows, shared pics on social media, and ate Bar Harbor delicacies. But I still felt a need for further satisfaction, which I knew would help quell the emotions that threatened to rise up.

The truth is, I was having a case of classic type Seven FOMO.

If you don't know about this type Seven trait, what the nine Enneagram types are, and why various types do what they do, don't worry, I'll give you an overview of each of the nine personality types soon! For now, let's just say that all the ice cream in the world couldn't cure the ache that lay deeply buried within me.

On the last day of our trip, these feelings were coming to a climax, so I developed a spontaneous plan as a sort of cure-all. We would have one final adventure, a crescendo that would create not only a diversion from my feelings but also an epic marriage and family memory.

"This path is a little too dull for me," I sang out to my family almost as soon as we got onto the beautiful but flat and very safe Ocean Path. The legendary adventure trail Beehive Mountain was in sight, and I had an idea brewing. "Let's just do a little bit of Beehive," I said, already moving ahead.

My husband groaned, as did one of my daughters, both of whom were aghast at the idea of starting another hike so soon—especially this formidable trek. When my husband verbalized that we were already on a beautiful route, the very one we had planned for this moment, I said, "I know, but we came to one of the most beautiful places in the world to have a real adventure. We'll go up the backside or just do a tiny bit. Plus, we'll literally have the rest of the day to lounge and eat ice cream."

The truth is, I wanted to be nice and tired before we sat down. Make that exhausted.

Since we didn't have a proper map, we asked directions from a father and son who had just come down the switchback at the trailhead. The father showed us there were two paths: one for easy and one for difficult. He told us to go right for the easy path.

It was left.

We went right, but we were on the wrong path. By the time we realized this, we had so quickly climbed up many slippery boulders that we could not turn back. There was also a sign that read, "One way only." It was virtually impossible to go down the same way we'd come up.

We soon found ourselves on the edge of a cliff with the clouds literally beneath us. There was still at least a half mile to go and also—gulp—iron rungs to climb ahead. Ahead of us, a family was stuck on those iron rungs, their little girl paralyzed with fear. None of us could get up if she didn't, so we all waited for her, and my middle child started to pick up on the girl's emotions and panic. We comforted her as best as we could.

As soon as we had clearance, my husband, an Enneagram One, pulled me aside to assess the situation critically. He reminded me that we had decided together in the hotel room that Beehive, clearly marked "Advanced" on the All Trails app, was not an option for our family's level of expertise. He further pointed out that the next sets of rungs looked like they had just been pounded into the mountain haphazardly, on top of the fact that we had very little water—just half a bottle for all of us in the heat. A debate started between us, and if I'm honest, I wanted to have it out right there. But we knew we had a problem to solve that was bigger than our personality differences.

Finally, after some careful assessing and gingerly steps, we made it to the top, safe and sound. We snapped a couple of plaque-at-the-summit pics and took a *lot* of deep breaths, letting the adrenaline roll off as we chatted with other hikers who had trekked the same harrowing adventure.

I am so grateful this family memory remains a happy one. While it was fraught at the time, the relief and joy of making it to the summit is the memory we keep with us. But that day was also a wake-up call for me personally. I realized that in my rush to burn steam and climb another dizzying height to discharge all my sadness and anxiety, I had endangered my people. That couldn't happen again.

Something would have to change.

That day, I decided it was time to delve further into my Enneagram work, but this time on a deeper level. I wanted to face my emotions squarely, allow tears in as necessary, and really let myself sit with my pain when it started to rise up. I decided to learn from some of the best and most emotionally wise Enneagram teachers in the world through podcasts, books, and interviews. Soaking in their wisdom, I shared what I'd heard on my new Instagram account for Enneagram and Marriage and did research with couples about their best lessons for moving through the world emotionally, mentally, and physically.

Since that fateful day on Beehive Mountain, I have learned so much from pausing to tend to my heart's aches instead of sheer overdoing. That has brought vast learning back into my life, marriage, and family after years of numbing out to my triggers. My husband has been doing his own work, and he has made more space for my emotions as well. With our tools and ongoing commitment to these balancing self-inventories and the awakening practices you will find in the pages of this book, we are stronger together and more intentionally shining brighter as individuals, as a couple, and as a family with one another and in the world.

I believe in the growth work you're stepping into here too. Will you join us in leaning toward balance and health with your spouse as you aim to shine brighter individually, together, and in your world? Will you start paying attention to the ways you truly bring the best and the worst out in each other? My friends, if you're brave in focusing on the journey in each chapter as well as in completing the questions that follow, you will truly bring one another forward into the light of your healthiest selves.

After two decades of walking my own path toward healing, I am even more passionate about helping couples learn their own and one another's best coping strategies, walking them through conflicts, helping them see one another's hearts, and offering them healthy, problem-solving strategies. Why? Because when they can see one another's truest vulnerabilities and fears and begin to trust one another with those exposed, raw places, it's right there that they feel safe enough to truly begin to grow.

As humans, we don't grow only individually. In marriage, we begin to combine our gifts and grow together to help the world in beautiful and unique ways—with the light of our unique relationship hues. As Carl Jung said, "The meeting of two personalities is like the contact of two chemical substances: if there is any reaction, both are transformed."[2]

The Marriage of Enneagram and Couples Therapy

The entire fields of both family systems therapy and social work are built around the premise that when we make intentional, healthy little shifts, we make a positive influence on one another on a personal, familial, and societal level. Doing our personal and relationship work matters so much more than we may realize.

What's more is that your impact as a couple comes full circle when you do some of your personal and marriage work as a unit, branching outward and bringing good things to the world. The Enneagram helps you to see how your particular light together shines out in unique angles.

Couples vary in the ways they shape the world. Sometimes they birth children together, they serve actively in communities together, they think critically together to solve problems, and they create projects and artistic expressions together. In other words, couples glow brightly when they're coloring the world with both the best of their individual essence and the best of their unique chemistry together.

As we begin the work of helping you understand both your own unique glow and the glow you can create alongside your partner, let me pause to answer a few questions.

What does the integration of two personality types mean for us and our relationship?

Don't worry, we're not going for codependence here but the understanding that together you create a sort of dance of interdependence and cast a light together. For instance, if you're in a relationship, think of your own essence as a mirrorball dangling in a dark room, shining out with its own particular light. As a new hue is cast upon you by your partner with their colorful gifts and traits, your own light emanates a little differently. (You can cue the Taylor Swift song "Mirrorball" here if you like!)

Finding your light together gives each of you more angles from which to shine out your best qualities. It helps the two of you serve the world better too. To romanticize it further, combining your best gifts with the best of your partner's gifts helps you to face the darkness you encounter in yourselves and in the world with the added luminescence—or, as I like to say, the "glow"—of your love together.

However (you knew this was sounding awfully idealistic), there's also a catch. We tend to lean into some of our partner's less refined qualities as well. We also bring our shadows to one another, taking on our partner's negative traits at times. And we can create a new shadow as a couple when we miss important things collectively. This can happen when we're not intentional with our personal, relational, and communal growth, such as when we try quick, instinctual fixes instead of actually facing the shadows of our lives squarely with wisdom, patience, and love.

This is why it's so important to marry the understanding of our personality types and our relationships. As you continue with me here, I'll show you how to blend with one another in a way that will truly allow you both to shine, as well as how to walk through your shadows in healthy ways across time.

Before we delve deeper (and we are delving deep, believe me!), let's start with the basics of the framework we'll be using to understand our personalities and our relationships: the Enneagram.

What exactly is the Enneagram?

You may know it as a trendy personality typing system that influencers use for creating memes and archetyping celebrities on their favorite sitcoms, but it's *so* much more than that. Although it's fun in popular culture to joke about our types or to debate whether Michael Scott on *The Office* is more like a type Two or a type Seven, it's also important to know that there are some compelling benefits that come from using the Enneagram as a personal, relational, and societal framework for growth. You may even have found this out for yourself by reading Ian Morgan Cron and Suzanne Stabile's very popular 2016 book, *The Road Back to You*.[3] Whether you're new to the Enneagram or just need a refresher, let me give you a brief summary of what it's all about.

The Enneagram is a system of personality integration that focuses on our core motivations, fears, strengths, and blind spots. The awareness we get from studying this system not only serves analytical insights but also provides emotional awareness and reminders of active growth tools we can use for our bodies. Unlike the many two-dimensional personality assessments that measure only mental traits, the Enneagram and the theories encompassing it offer a more robust system that allows growth to unfold in our lives with a healthy balancing of the body, heart, mind, and even spirit.

So why is it called the Enneagram?

The name comes from the Greek words *ennea*, which means nine, and *gramma*, which means something that's drawn or written. The symbol of the Enneagram comes from ancient mathematics studied across cultures and over time.[4] It consists of an inner triangle and another triangular figure called a hexad connecting all the numbered points to one another with various arrows and lines, alluding to the fact that our personality types are not meant to be fixed but have movement and dimension.

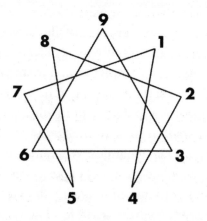

The Enneagram system focuses on sorting or "typing" people into these numbered points, with each number having its own unique motivations, fears, and internal dynamics. If it sounds a bit like the Sorting Hat in Harry Potter, maybe it is, but only on the surface. Instead of just the four houses of Hogwarts, there are nine Enneagram types. These types have been studied for millennia in some form or other in an attempt to systematize and order the complexities of humanity at least to some degree.

The Enneagram was not authored by just one person but instead has been an ongoing human collaboration of individuals trying to understand one of the biggest questions of all time: How do we come to understand the human psyche and the ways we grow in mind, body, heart, and spirit? Some of the most notable Enneagram scholars are Oscar Ichazo and Claudio Naranjo, who drew from Gurdjieff and even from Plato, Plotinus, and the Desert Fathers.[5] The late Don Riso and many in the Jesuit order spent much time in the 1970s and 1980s developing the typology further, and many since have also added to the research, notably Beatrice Chestnut, Uranio Paes, Helen Palmer, Russ Hudson, the late Dr. David Daniels, and Peter O'Hanrahan.

Like the four ancient temperaments of Hippocrates[6] or any truly rigorous modern personality system, the purpose of the Enneagram is to understand ourselves so we will make decisions that will better us and our relationships in every area of life. In fact, at the end of the day, we want to look a little *less* obviously like one rigid personality type so we don't just get stamped with a meme and passed over. That, of course, is personality typing at its worst, so please don't do this branding to your spouse or yourself.

Remember, we want to grow, to change, and to adapt as we work on our own intrapsychic dynamics. We want to learn from one another's typology, gifts, insights, and experiences. We don't want to use a type or number to box someone in, to make them feel worse than someone else, or to make them feel like they can never grow or shift. However, knowing the type or types with which we most and least identify can and does help us to understand our growth process more specifically.

The images of the Enneagram in this book are just to give you an idea of the flow of the system and are ultimately incomplete, as are all drawings of something theoretical. This is in part because theories are never fully understood, but also because the Enneagram isn't just a flat, circular drawing with points. It is a robust, spherical symbol of the interplay of all the types with their fluidity and underpinnings, and we continue to learn more as we collectively study.

That doesn't mean there isn't much for you to learn about yourself and your partner. The pieces of the Enneagram system that we will be discussing in this book have already been greatly developed. I've also integrated truths I've learned from two decades of study in the fields of psychology, marriage, and human development.

It's important to note that there are no perfect pairings within the Enneagram system. There are no pairs that are more or less compatible. The truth is, romantic as I am, I know that *all* healthy relationships have strengths and weaknesses and take work. So if you're questioning whether you're paired up well with your partner in terms of your personality type, let me assure you.

Any type can work well with any other type.

Yes, truly! There are no bad pairings. So go ahead and take a deep breath. You and your spouse are not the "wrong personality types" for one another because there *is* no wrong type.

In fact, each couple, whatever their personality types are, creates their own unique chemistry together as the elements of each person's essence and personality combine. They blend their gifts and traits like threads of a tapestry interwoven, exposing and grafting in shades and patterns that were not seen in each person individually before.

If the Enneagram and marriage growth aren't about compatibility, how will doing our personal and relationship work in this book influence our relationship?

In addition to learning about how your type influences others and how you shine together, you'll find new routes to growing together that seem small but actually make a big difference in your everyday life together.

When we intentionally learn about the particular movements that help each type grow, we can take small steps instead of staying stuck in the same rigid patterns and defense mechanisms of our own type all the time. Learning from our spouses' and others' types at their best also helps us to expand our own frame of reference and find different and often healthier ways of doing things. This is the work I'm excited to walk you through!

Think about each person in a relationship as an element in a chemistry experiment of sorts. Just as when we combine two hydrogen atoms with one oxygen atom to make something beyond each of those elements alone—something necessary for life (H_2O!)—so it is when two humans combine elementally. They have the potential to burn brightly and make beautiful new displays of creation together.

This is a reminder that our Enneagram-type gifts not only *can* combine but *need* to combine for the world to go round well. We all have a role to play in this lifetime that we are caught up in together "for such a time as this," as the ancients would say.

Whether married or single, we need to figure out how to be team players. We *all* benefit when one of us is doing well. Thus, knowing our Enneagram types helps us to learn our gifts and struggles, and it aids us in working as a collective versus withdrawing into ourselves or ranking our gifts higher or lower than others'. Instead of misusing our gifts, casting a dark shadow on the world, or bowing out altogether, we can—we *must*—find our Enneagram Glow.

What is my Enneagram type?

As someone who used to conduct complex psychological assessments before using the Enneagram to help couples grow healthier, I'm confident the Enneagram is among the very best of psychological tools. Now I'll assist you in finding your type (or refreshing you on your type) and its traits. Even if you think you already know all about yourself and your spouse, read on. Some people, experts included, have mistyped themselves or their spouses, so it's important to make sure you're attuned to yourself and to one another as you begin.

For now, let's start with just a brief description of how each of the nine types work as they present both individually and in the context of a relationship. While it's ideal to find a type you resonate most with for the purposes of growth, it's okay if you resemble more than one type in this initial read-through, or even if you find a bit of yourself in all the types. As you progress through this book, you'll pick up new teachings about each of the types, which will help clarify things in time.

The Nine Types

In your typology study, remember not to "sort" away or withdraw from one another by overly classifying or polarizing yourself or your spouse. Also, make sure you don't reduce someone down to just their type. As with all labels, use person-first language. Each of us is a person before a numerical title or a type of any kind. Be kind as you explore your questions and as you work together to find personal and relational health.

Type Ones are often known for their goodness and their tendency toward editing or improving others and themselves. They may have a perfectionistic slant, which is usually designated to a few areas of life and not implemented everywhere. They enjoy making high-quality, detailed investments in others and in themselves and are often moralistic. Additionally, they are sensory oriented, noticing sights, sounds, smells, tastes, and touches with great nuance. They love to do things to completion and without waste. They often experience joy and relief at the mere act of doing something well or being perceived as good by the culture. They are often concerned so much with keeping to their strict inner code that they worry they are hopelessly bad or wrong if they make any mistake at all.

In marriage, they love to find a spouse who shares their desire to bring healthy structure, order, and goodness to the world and to their families. They are logical and good listeners. They value hard work before play, as it gives them inner permission to laugh and to let go, which often allows an unfolding of their deep hearts of love and artistry.

Type Twos are often noted as major contributors and generous givers in their families and cultures. They love to find special places in their communities to serve others. Nothing else brings them more inner harmony than knowing they are close to and in good standing with those they 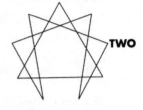 love. They need to be reminded of this often. They are greatly attuned to the needs of the world around them and are not afraid to talk to their spouses and peers about things of depth, naturally welcoming these topics in with nurture and comfort. Often they don't take time to do their own emotional processing because they are so busy finding worth through serving in the world, enjoying pleasurable experiences, and serving their family.

In marriage, they love to find a spouse who both understands their heart to nurture and their desire to save the world. Ideally, they want to bring their partner along for service projects and times of connection or at least to be given the freedom to give of themselves. If introverted, they will want most of this special time to be just for the two of them and in smaller groups. They also love it when they feel like their spouse is a strong support they can lean on after their long, hard days. Most of all, they love to be adored by their spouse. This helps them to define their worth, even as they try to remember that inner worth is inherent.

Type Threes are often seen as excellent performers and achievers in workspaces, community groups, and whatever public spaces they find value in. Threes can be perfectionistic, going to almost any length to do things with excellence. They love to fit in at the top of the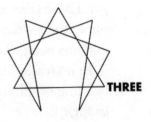

cultural echelon and to passionately pursue whatever is the reigning paradigm for success and acceptance. They truly want their achievements to be noteworthy, not just for goodness' sake but so they can gain the love they need and desire.

In marriage, they love being both admired and leaned on for support in almost every capacity. In addition to wanting a loyal connection, they deeply want their spouse to love them for who they are on the inside, even when they're relaxing or vulnerable. At their core, they worry this is not the case and thus deceive themselves—and sometimes others—to make sure they are seen as successful and on top of their game.

Type Fours are often viewed as artists, individualists, and dreamers. They spend time in contemplative spaces of depth and intricate understanding, both in their own minds and in the artistry they bring to the world. Fours are good at leading others into vulnerable spaces of depth on an intimate level. They can show compassion and give others permission to be in process or flawed

FOUR

yet still beloved. They enjoy shared understanding that comes from suffering and yet surviving together. At their core, they worry that they have a fatal flaw and that unless they are unique and do a bit of a wistful push-pull dance with their loved ones, they will be resigned to a bleak fate of loneliness or even self-loathing.

In marriage, they long for a spouse who will let them share their honesty, woes, and wounds and stay there with them for a time, as well as rise with them into deep joy. They also want a spouse who recognizes their dislike for being boxed in or feeling too average and thus being potentially insignificant. Though they often resist being understood, they hope someone will take large amounts of time to love and understand them, even as they find out they too are flawed.

Type Fives are often viewed as researchers and investigators as they spend time exploring and innovating in their interior world. As such, they are often introverted and prefer to keep their groups of friends separate from one another. Fives love to focus deeply, tinker with systems, and find out why things work the way they do.

FIVE

They can display an air of conceit once they have achieved a level of mastery, though they often struggle with self-doubt about whether they have really learned enough to jump into situations safely or with enough energy. They can get lost in any number of research projects or fandom, to the extent that they have trouble coming out of these fantasies or wormholes and relating to the outside world again.

In marriage, they desire a spouse who realizes that they need time and space for their version of R and R (rest and research), especially considering the real or perceived lack of energy that they face daily. They also hope they can be loved despite dealing with the inner struggle of incompetency. Yet their intelligence in most cases makes them one of the most competent people in their circles of influence or fields of study.

Type Sixes are often seen as caring, loyal troubleshooters, able to find problems, tackle them, and cautiously move forward, step by careful step. Sixes are a bit of a paradox in their quest for trust. They can test others quite a lot. They tend to be skeptical of

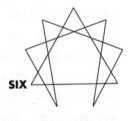

SIX

trusting both themselves and others, as they have seen things go sideways in life and want to be well prepared. They can get quite reactive about this planning desire, especially since they care so very deeply about doing what is right for themselves and their people. Though full of doubts, they ultimately love to find leaders in their circle whom they can turn to when their very analytical minds begin to spin too far into anxiety and fear.

In marriage, Sixes want a spouse who will both understand and support them in their concerns, who will allow them to make plans because of their troubleshooting nature, and who will let them share their fears and concerns regularly. They also desire a trustworthy, caring spouse who will ultimately empower them to walk away from the unhealthy cowardice that often holds them back from their beautiful courage. They long for and are thrilled by someone who will challenge them to grow in wisdom and to take healthy risks.

Type Sevens are known as enthusiasts and encouragers, and when grounded, they can excel at creative problem-solving with their quick minds and optimistic solutions. Inquisitive by nature, Sevens love to revel in their creative imaginations and  drink of the pleasures of life, encouraging others in the drinking of wellness also. They feel best when gaining pleasure and freedom and by satisfying the external senses. This Epicurean posture of curiosity and imagination at times aids them in avoiding the anxieties and essential tasks of life and their deepest feelings. When their whirling, always-busy mind and body stop in exhaustion, the Seven must deal with their inner pain, boredom, consequences, and dark or terrifying feelings like everyone else. When they do, they learn that they can face them and emerge with an open heart, sobered and focused.

In marriage, Sevens want a spouse who will give them freedom to explore but also challenge them to live with moderation, rest, and care since they often keep an unsustainable pace. On a deeper level, they desire someone who is trustworthy with their sensitive though buried hearts, as well as someone who can hold their pain with them for just a little while and encourage them not to run from hard things.

Type Eights are often thought of as the protectors and challengers of the world, in that they deeply care for the underprivileged. They also want to make sure that those they love feel defended and passionately loved by them. Eights love to enjoy life on a grand, experiential level

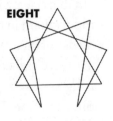

EIGHT

with their sensual natures and love the finest experiences life can offer, indulging in them for hours at a time. They often quite naturally find a willing tribe to lead with their practical, stoic leadership (or even dominance), although this can sometimes make others afraid of their strong pull. Eights do not like being vulnerable with their feelings unless it is with someone they can trust, and even then, they are often reticent until there is complete assurance of an alliance proved across time and much testing.

In marriage, Eights love a spouse who sees their huge heart underneath their strong exterior and who will match their strength in some capacity. Eights want someone who will rise to the occasion with specific, desired acts of love and loyalty, to support them in the same way they long to support their spouse—to the fullest capacity, at all costs.

Type Nines are the calmest of the types and yet still extremely strong, with enough potential energy to be revolutionaries. They typically spend much of their time resting, being peacekeepers, or being mildly diplomatic. A Nine in growth is a marvel to see. Paired with their strength is a deep love—they often carry great regard or care

NINE

for the personhood of everyone on earth. They fear that they don't matter and that their voice will be unheard. Therefore, sometimes they distance themselves completely, going into a "turtle shell" of comfort—harboring hurts and protecting their basic human material desires—since they worry their upper-level feelings will not be met.

In marriage, Nines desire a spouse who will honor them, offer them direction and options, and help them prioritize themselves, their self-care, and their comfort, the latter of which greatly matters to them. They get internally upset when they have worked hard to sacrifice and to understand and merge with others who in turn do not support or listen to them. They also want someone who will support their justice-oriented causes and rally with them for peaceable, active changes in the world.

Now that you've read about the nine types, you're likely starting to have an idea of what your strengths and areas for growth are in your relationship. It's time to talk about the ways you can truly help one another to shine out of your gifts as you combine them.

In addition to your typology relationship health and stress, I will share a bit about complementary types that are helpful for the various types to learn from. These complementary types are called the wings and arrows. Each person has a main Enneagram type as well as two complementary arrow types and two complementary wing types. It's important that you don't let wings and arrows distract you from your main type's work but that you use them as a deeper-dive aid for growth.

Arrows

Each of the primary nine Enneagram types has two other types connected to it by way of arrows. The arrow pointing toward each type is what some Enneagram experts call the starting or growth point. The arrow pointing away from the type is an end or resolution point, a final move for the person to take for a more completely healthy self. For example, Enneagram Four is the starting point for an individual who is a type Two, while Enneagram Eight is the resolution point. The concept of arrows potentially has many layers, but in general, the connected arrow types offer a mini treatment plan as a guide for the growth an individual does.

Why add other types into the mix? In general, the more integrated we are with the other types, the more we become a balanced and functional human. For instance, if someone relates as an Enneagram Four and tends to be slower paced and introspective, it's important for them to use their One arrow to get moving and organized as well as their Two arrow to get them thinking of and helping others. If you don't know much about your arrow types, I encourage you to read about them also.

Wings

There are two more points that are helpful as you view your type, and these are the types on either side of yours. These points are known as the Enneagram wings, since we exhibit traits not only from our types but also from the neighboring types. In addition to the analogy of butterfly wings opening for smoother takeoff into maturity, I like to use the analogy of shades of colors when it comes to type and wings, especially as we think of the Enneagram Glow concept. If a type Six is thought of as yellow, for instance, then its wings would direct us to nearby colors on the spectrum, such as orange (type Five traits) and green (type Seven traits). Your life is, of course, colored in with more shades and nuances, but when you allow yourself to use shades or aspects of the Enneagram map, you have more options for shining out all the brighter.

When it comes to wings, most people find that there's usually a stronger, or dominant, wing instead of a precise balance between the two. The wing is often notated as a *w* following a person's core type. For instance, if someone identifies as an Enneagram Six, they are said to have a Five wing and a Seven wing. If they lean farther to the Five traits, such as research and focus, than to the Seven traits, such as enthusiasm and extroversion, they are said to have a Six wing Five (6w5 in shorthand). If someone is a Two, their wings are One and Three.

Remember, the goal is to stop leaning so hard to one side or the other but to balance the traits of the core type as well as both wings.

How Do We Influence One Another's Types?

When I was in my third year of working with Enneagram couples from a family systems framework, I started to notice patterns. Not only were couples of similar pairings alike, but couples were different from others of their own type because they were merging with their spouse's type. For example, a Two married to a Three was often very different from a Two married to a Nine.

I most noticeably observed this pattern in the type Two and the type Five dance of marriage as I saw the couple merging in ways a bit different from my typical experiences with them as individuals. Over time, the Five was allowing the Two's love and nurture to fill them with more confidence, fueling their competency with their need for love. Likewise, the Five's playful desire to keep the Two close and at home was reminding the Two of their love and worth even without their service. The Five also helped the Two spend more time at rest and taught them to enjoy their own company, though this was certainly not an easy journey for the Two (hence why this pairing, a fun combination when in balance, typically contacts me). To my joy, I also saw Twos and Fives with other types grow in other wonderful ways across time, each sharpened by their mate in a myriad of ways, regardless of what their partner's gifts were.

I was witnessing in couples the important truth that it isn't just nature or genes that determine our personality. Indeed, nurture and environment also play a large role in adding layers and complexity to our self-development. I sought to determine whether this concept was seen in other Enneagram work and asked those I saw as leaders about it.

I found that this concept of layering, or taking on the traits of surrounding individuals, had been studied before in the context of families and cultures. Many Enneagram scholars have also theorized on family overlays.[7] For instance, if your father was a careful One, you may more likely be One-ish yourself or even mistake yourself as a One, even though at your core you have other main issues and gifts. Similarly, if your workplace has the vibe of achieving relentlessly, like an Enneagram Three does, or has a research-based Five-ish culture, you often feel the pressure to follow suit.

Geographically, if you came from Rio de Janeiro, Brazil, you may often note an overlay of a passionate, joyful Seven-ish persona that has rubbed off from your culture. You may be a Four-ish person if you come from France, often thought of as a romantic culture, even though you're higher in Enneagram Eight gifts. In this way, you may have Seven-ish or Four-ish tendencies while still not being a Seven or a Four.

As you can see, the capacity for layering is not limited to influencing your partner's personality attributes. In fact, couples can also help one another heal from trauma, even without typology. The trauma therapist on my team, Glenda Reagan, helps me see this when she talks about how we can heal one another's wounds in marriage. I find that we often seek partners who differ from us, sometimes in quite opposite ways. There is a likelihood that instinctively we understand that they have gifts we do not yet possess but wish to, gifts we especially hope that our community or potential offspring will possess as we try to heal one another's wounds.

One may ask, would we eventually find our way without these gifts and without these influences, namely our spouses? Community is part of survival, and these overlays are all a bit of a complex pattern. It is anecdotally said, however, that it was the one-to-one bond that got the Holocaust survivors through the Nazi regime. There's definitely an important value for the growth we offer to our partners, despite the fact that sometimes we grow on our own. You don't need a partner to ensure you become more generous, but it sure does help to have community and the close bonds of family and friends who can rub off on and support one another across time.

My Hope for You

The rest of the Enneagram teachings, exercises, and tools in this book are integrated with spiritual wisdom and reputable marriage research with the utmost care. I have engaged with thousands of individuals in the process of preparing for this journey together, and it's my complete honor and privilege to have this seat next to you for the journey.

My ultimate hope as you read this book is that you find refreshment as you become a healthier individual, that you find grace and understanding for your spouse, and most of all, that you find the unique way you can shine together in the world with your unique Enneagram pairing.

Your spouse does not have to read this book with you. However, if they do decide to embark on the journey with you, my hopes are even greater because I know that together you will shine brighter than ever!

Finally, I want to thank you for the hard work and soul-searching you're planning to do with me in the following pages. I respect and applaud you for that brave step of hope you're taking for your relationship. May these insights, tips, and tools guide you along the way.

Happy glowing!

How to Read This Book

However you choose to move through these pages, whether individually, as a couple, or as a group with others, do it with a plan and with focus. Write down the action steps you plan to take and ask for accountability with another reader or mentor. I've been coaching for almost two decades now, and I know that writing down your intentions and sharing them with others who care about you makes a *huge* difference.

If you need help defining any of the terms as we trek together, be sure to turn to the glossary on page 269. You'll create an even healthier relationship culture as you build upon your unique story together with clarifying terms. Feel free to discard any glossary terms that distract you from the work you're doing, and take one thoughtful step of growth at a time.

At the end of each chapter, you will find three sections under the heading "Afterglow." These sections will lead you into a practical engagement of your bodies, minds, and hearts, so you can allow the materials from the chapter to settle in and bring you forward in a healthy way.

Illuminate: This section will offer you tips to think through as you begin to examine your own life through the lens of a thoughtful observer.

Spark Up Heart-to-Heart Conversation: This section offers questions for you to answer individually and potentially together as you consider how to safely open up your hearts to one another.

Glow Brightly Together: This section contains assignments for you and your partner to try to stoke the fires of love with strength and vibrancy together.

AFTERGLOW

Illuminate: Which of the types do you relate to the most? Ask your spouse which one they relate to the most, even if they aren't reading the book with you. Don't push or label them, but gently inquire.

Spark Up Heart-to-Heart Conversation: Which of the types you studied, if any, generates a strong emotion of some sort, like weariness, anger, or sadness? Spend a few moments journaling about it or talking it out with your spouse.

Glow Brightly Together: What can you do to use the gifts of your type to encourage your partner this week? Get the process rolling by doing something kind right now.

1

The Stages of Your Enneagram Glow across Time

They can only come to the morning through the shadows.

J. R. R. Tolkien[1]

"You should really give Wes a chance," my friend Heather said to me as we slammed our lockers at Harry S. Truman High School between classes.

Heather was assertive and even a bit audacious to confront me with love so boldly in my new singlehood. I appreciated her direct nature, even if I was more reserved with my heart.

"No way! He's not my type," I replied.

As I had observed from a few past experiences, Wes and I were completely different types of people and from vastly different families as well. Though we were both well-known in student government and other clubs, we were at opposite ends of the spectrum when it came to just about everything.

Wes was a classic jock from a Southern family. He lived on one of the only farms in Taylor, Michigan, as I had discovered the year before when my former boyfriend and I had given him a ride home. For fun, he enjoyed working on his old hot rod or playing football. He was quarterback and captain of the football team. I was pretty sure he was the president of the Bible club too.

Though I loved athletics, I had a desire for sports that emphasized self-reliance and a rich interior. (In other words, I had self-esteem issues and this was my workaround.) I kept moving all the time. I had a season pass at the local ski lodge, ran 5Ks just for fun outside of my track meets, and was captain of the girls' tennis team. I relied on myself and my curated clique of friends exclusively for a sense of identity and safety in an unforgivably large herd.

But Wes—with his pickup truck and all-American good looks, at the top of the class, attending church three times a week in between football practices and farm duties—did not seem to notice these opposing forces. Or if he did, he didn't let them stop him from pursuing me.

On paper and by my quick analysis, Wes and I seemed so wrong for each other. However, when he started pursuing me in our literature class, somewhere between *A Farewell to Arms* and Mark Twain's antics along the Mississippi, I was shocked to realize I began to actually like him—a lot. So I did what any young type Seven does when emotions run high and love comes knocking on her door.

I ran.

I didn't save him a dance at the Sadie Hawkins event like he asked, and I managed to skirt the hallways every time he showed up. He didn't quite catch up with me until he found me singing Christmas carols at a nursing home during a student leadership outing a few months later. That fateful night, I stayed extra late to visit each patient, and he offered me a ride home. I brought Heather along and even made her sit in the seat between us in his truck.

When he dropped her off first and finally asked me to join him for a movie date, I reluctantly said yes.

The date was an epic fail at first. When he picked me up, this clean-cut traditional young man was greeted by a depressive girl smelling of incense and wearing thrift store corduroys, a huge brown wool sweater, and first-generation Vans. (I was in the absolute height of my alternative grunge phase.) I wondered at his careful driving, his cowboy boots, and his full mustache. (Yes, you read that right—full mustache at sixteen.) However, after the movie, he asked me the most endearing question, one that would change our lives forever as we stepped into our place in history and into destiny together.

"Would you like to go somewhere to talk and to have a piece of pie?"

What happened at Denny's that night was even sweeter than pie to me. He really did just want to talk, and that spoke to me. Conversation for the sake of conversation was a foreign concept to me at the time. Most kids in my town, including me, had something rebellious on their minds, be it alcohol, marijuana, or sex.

So, talk we did, all through the night. By giving him a chance, I found that he was innocent, trusting, and good. I was so taken aback by his manners and care that I felt unable to resist spending more time with him.

We've been together ever since that day, twenty-seven years ago.

While we didn't have the words to articulate it at the time, we were a match of opposites: a One and a Seven. One month into our relationship, we were influencing each other in all kinds of ways. I began to pour feminine nurture into his life and helped to fill him with confidence. I'm sorry to say my influence was not all this good. I planned the biggest school-skipping event in history since *Ferris Bueller's Day Off*, and to my surprise, Wes, who desperately needed more youthful passion and spontaneity in his serious life, came along. (As a morally upright type One, he

37

did ask parental permission first.) I also helped him to designate one weekend night each week for time with friends. He came out with my friends and me after football games and just enjoyed a night on the town being a teenager, even though he wasn't doing anything wild.

Lo and behold, Wes began to rub off on me too. In the spring of my junior year, at his prodding, I started to pay attention more in school. I even began to attend my honors precalculus lectures, to Mr. Poole's delight, instead of conveniently getting out of class for student government duties and cramming it all in sloppily and late.

Wes also supported my love of psychology and literature. I told him I read the classics at night, something I'd never confessed to anyone. He even suggested we hang out with my parents, even though their idea of fun was writing poetry, watching *Jeopardy*, and doing the *Reader's Digest* vocabulary quizzes. For the first time, my own literary interests were appealing to someone. Thanks to him, I began to see more value in them as opposed to simply carrying adolescent shame about them.

I began to find more academic accolades coming my way again, as I had in earlier years when life was more innocent. Though my friends were caring in other ways, they had written me off as their wild, fun friend and told me my college board scores, winning Voice of Democracy speeches, and moments of academic attention were total flukes. They weren't trying to be mean; I had likewise written off my abilities, as many immature and unfocused teens are prone to do. Wes, however, encouraged and celebrated these things in me.

We kept influencing one another through the years of engagement and marriage. I ended up graduating from college and graduate school with honors and pursuing a career I always knew I was made for. I later put Wes through medical school and encouraged him to finish even though he felt on many days that he just wasn't good enough. I can still remember calling him up one day to tell him I got him into the class he needed at Oakland University after the registrar had told him he was too late.

I bet you can relate to this early season together in a relationship. Even though there are often things to work through from the beginning, this stage can be a beautiful season of elements combining—a season when you and your partner champion one another in ways no one else ever has. Maybe your friend circles and your life trajectories dramatically shift, and your ways of walking through the world are more vibrant and colorful. New couples are really winning with these added and unexpected new hues being grafted in from one another's gifts and ways of moving through the world.

However, as time goes on, that "glow" created in the beginning begins to look very different. As it turned out, being voted "cutest couple," being on homecoming court together, and having hard-earned scholarships could only take Wes and me so far. Those early differences and questions I had asked about how a relationship with such disparity would work out later demanded answers. Perhaps you've come to the same realization in your own relationship.

No one in those early stages can be expected to comprehend the allegorical Robert Frost poem "Nothing Gold Can Stay."[2] We instead insist that it will always be dawn. This early spring of a relationship carries us far, as it should. Yet as our own relationship continued, Wes and I encountered the frost.

If a marriage lasts long enough, every couple will experience seasons of shadow. Then the worst of their types come at them, losses awaken them to the deepest pain imaginable, unexpected illnesses ensue, and perhaps even crises of faith take place. Though the shifts will be different for everyone, all couples will find themselves in the shadows if they're together long enough. Digging in and doing their work helps so much in times like this. As J. R. R. Tolkien reminds us, "Deep roots are not reached by the frost."[3]

Whatever stage of a relationship you're in right now—early attraction, young love, or later shadows—I want you to know there is so much more than that basic chemistry we initially find together. I want you to know about all the phases of a dynamic relationship so you can find your deepest, richest, most authentic way of lighting up the world together. Then you can find that, though nothing gold can stay, your roots are deep and there is purpose and even beauty in *all* seasons. There are indeed riches, even as all that is gold does not glitter.

I am deeply passionate about helping you through this experience. After walking through so many heights, depths, and shadows myself and working with thousands of couples over the last two decades, I've noticed patterns and seasons that are part of it all. As I integrated the Enneagram into my work, I began to call these seasons the "Stages of the Enneagram Glow." The Enneagram Glow is simply the name surrounding the idea that we cast both lights and shadows together when in a long-term relationship or marriage.

As you walk through these stages, it's of utmost importance to realize that though you can expect some linear growth, life is often found between the margins. Thus, these phases often overlap. Cutting or spiraling through them in various spiderweb patterns across spans of life is normal and expected.

There is implicit good news here. You don't need to wait till you're eighty to hit the afterglow season of life. Indeed, my hope is that you will be thriving together sooner rather than later and as frequently as possible! By knowing that seasons come and go in life and marriage, you're less wrapped up in the "why" of finding yourself in various tangled-up moments and more focused on finding your very best route through together.

To help you understand the stages of the Enneagram Glow, I've summarized what you can generally expect in each stage of a relationship and included an example of how one couple glows together as they've walked through the years. What's more, in "The Glow Pairing Dictionary" in the back of this book, you can find your own pairing's unique stages of the Enneagram Glow across time.

Once again, please understand there are varieties even within each type, as you each have your own neural pathways, memories, and experiences that shape you. Still, each of these stages is representative of stages most couples will go through at one time or another. It's helpful to see where you've been and where you are heading if you're intentional with your growth journey.

Enneagram Glow Stage 1: Shine

Two people find one another and decide they will pair up. Their instincts and types move in beautiful ways together. They love one another for who they are and who they will become. Each is satisfied and blessed with the work their partner has done at an early point and decides their mutual gifts will carry them far into the next generation of healthy influence. A quote from Jane Austen's book *Persuasion* sums up this stage so well: "There could have been no two hearts so open, no tastes so similar, no feelings so in unison."[4]

> Luke and Emma were an opposites-attract pairing: types Three and Five. They found great harmony and juncture in their grand but wise plans for carrying out life. Luke, the Three, began to feel permission to rest with Emma, the Five, instead of going at an all-out sprint both at work and at home. Emma began to show her vast intelligence more with support and encouragement from Luke, who also began realizing he was allowed to make

41

more detailed plans. Instead of unhealthily colluding with their vastly different experiences from childhood, Luke and Emma marveled that they had each found a partner who had gifts they did not possess. This offered them refreshment and hope for healing.

Enneagram Glow Stage 2: Heal

A couple realizes that their partner has wounds that they can help to heal with their particular gifts, and there is a multifaceted impact. They reach out to one another in support through early trials, and they set boundaries with family, at work, and in whatever ways they choose. They begin building a family or community with mutual gifts and developing a sense of safety together.

> Luke learned that Emma, an only child, had been given the task of keeping her single mother company as a parentified adult figure of sorts. He was aghast that she'd had to take on so much emotional duress so young, so he helped her set boundaries with her extended family and shouldered some of the burden as well, helping her family get their lives in order. Emma also began dealing with her underlying fears and taking time to secure the couple's finances, which allowed them to live comfortably and enjoy vacations just for fun. She began to feel like she had purpose. She in turn helped Luke by cheering for him in his job as a financial adviser as he climbed the ladder of corporate success. They rose to the top in their businesses and their personal finances and helped many people.

Enneagram Glow Stage 3: Shadows and Throwing Shade

A couple forgets the ways they healed one another and begins to think they have gotten healthier independently. In reality, their partner has typically helped to support them in some ways. They realize that doing their work together is much harder the busier life gets. One or both get stuck in deeper defense mechanisms since stress is greater with time and trials. Each person uses specific defense strategies instead of doing the hard and painful work of leaving poor coping strategies behind. Neither party wants to admit that the very things they once enjoyed about each other now annoy them. Conflict mounts. They feel they've been burned, not blessed. They continue to discount their partner's role in helping them along.

This is where a fixed mindset can be disastrous. If the couple can't pivot here, it's difficult to save the marriage.

> Several years down the road, Luke felt like now that Emma had found her fortress at home in terms of securing finances and setting boundaries, she was shutting down even toward him emotionally. This was partly true, since she did enjoy her quiet life quite a bit. Plus, as a Five, Emma was fairly self-sufficient and did her own jobs from home, which increasingly brought her a fluid income. Luke felt proud but also a bit threatened by his prior role shifting. He also found Emma increasingly aggressive when they argued, which surprised him since she was typically introverted.
>
> Emma in turn felt like Luke's bold Three nature and sometimes emotional attention-seeking had unnecessarily disrupted the quiet one too many times. In truth, he was very jealous of her time away from him and was deeply insecure, as his big heart was feeling wounded. He also found himself testing her in various ways.
>
> They were both retreating and contemplating divorce, hurt by the ways their spouse had not done their inner work and dismayed that the very traits they had once been admired for were now loathed.[5]

Enneagram Glow Stage 4: Immerse

A couple takes time to do their personal self-care and relationship work, and in most cases, they turn to God for help in climbing out of the shadows. In this space they look not just at their partner's shadows but also at their own. This is especially necessary as their once-helpful coping strategies have all but ruined their life. They realize that while they must grieve who their partner is not, the best parts of their partner may still be there. Perhaps there is even more growth ahead. The work is slow and at times painful but worth the refining process.

> Doing their inner work with a coach gave Luke and Emma time and perspective to grow. Luke realized that his Three energy was indeed relentless in pursuit and, in that respect, daunting to Emma. She retreated when she felt it, especially since at times his retributive energy seemed to lead him to shadow living even regarding the smallest, unintentional offenses. In the past, her boundaries had never seemed to matter to her already-stressed attachment figures (her mother), and it felt like the pursuer-distancer cycle was relentless.
>
> Emma eventually realized that while she had set some good boundaries, she had gone inward so far that she was leaving her husband in the dust to cope alone, when all he really wanted was her encouraging perspective.
>
> When the couple began to compassionately learn about one another's styles of coping, Luke's demands decreased, and Emma more intentionally addressed them when they did surface. Together, they could now work out what was important.

Enneagram Glow Stage 5: Glow 2.0 (or Sunrise)

A couple realizes that with inner growth, their collective gifts are shining brighter than ever. They are well aware of strengths and weaknesses. The couple adapts to life with healthier boundaries as the walking wounded together. They don't burden their spouse with expectations only God can meet, yet they may lament their partner's failings at times, which is normal. They are committed to ongoing growth and balance together with their unique glow and gifts as a couple. They not only shine out their lights of love toward one another, but they're also becoming aware of how they may cast a shadow on the world collectively. They're actively taking steps to remove this barrier so they can carry their life and legacy even farther together. In this stage, spouses have the potential to become like the best of one another as they pull the other along and keep each other from making grave mistakes that they may be more prone to make on their own.

> Luke and Emma found their stride by working on their issues together over time. They took breaks in between for fitness and created times for fun indulgences, intimacy, and date nights. They emerged shining brightly, like they had at the beginning of their relationship, but they had a new hue. Their combined work created an even greater impact on others, who watched them soften into a bright glow together.
>
> Emma has some Three vibrancy that is a part of her even without Luke, while Luke has allowed the thoughtful countenance of his Five wife to give him permission to delve into, take time on, or even finish projects. He now rests well, not in denial but with a true calmness. He's also a better diplomat at home and at work. Emma makes sure she takes the brave steps to engage with him in some way every day so she isn't lost to research or planning. Emma's mother, whom they once wrote off as a poor, undignified woman who mistreated them, has gained respect in their life and is seen as an individual with her own traumas and scars. However, Emma and Luke set appropriate boundaries with her as well.

Enneagram Glow Stage 6: Afterglow

A couple does ongoing maintenance work as needed, celebrates their gifts, and continues to sharpen their lives together with ongoing self-care and time for their relationship. Often they speak into the lives of other couples and in their community with a vibrancy and compassion not seen before. They are also mature and mindful enough to know the shadows that may creep in and the ways they as a couple may have blind spots. They continue to immerse themselves in the work as needed and to integrate the best of all nine types. They know it's important to address their work in an active, ongoing fashion, even as they enjoy the flow of reciprocal love.

Luke and Emma now do maintenance work with their therapist once a month. They enjoy their weekly date nights and work to support one another's dreams as a Three-Five pairing. They have individual mentors as well as a couple of safe friends they both like and respect in their support group.

Emma ended up going back to school to become a professor. They welcomed a child into the mix and are beyond exhausted, but Luke was able to begin consulting so he could set his own hours efficiently, thanks to his bodywork, support, and stability at home. Luke and Emma care for each other's hearts with shared love, logic, and healthy boundaries and bring a spark to almost everything they do, even as they're actively working out conflict and giving each day's ultimate plans to God.

As we take a backseat view of the trajectory of this couple while they walked through all the stages of their relationship, we find the specific ways they've created a beautiful, lasting love and influence together. In the simplest of terms, now Emma is a very Three-ish Five and Luke is a very Five-ish Three. They still possess their individual gifts, but there are also new elements that will be a lasting part of each of them. Their hard work has paid off in a number of ways.

My hope is that your hard work will pay off in the same way.

Remember, the stages are not perfectly linear. Rather, they're a guide for us when we fall off course. For instance, you may find yourself in the final stage quite young and remain there for many years. Alternatively, in life's ebbs and flows (and glows!), you may find yourself needing another round of immersion, where you lean into the basics and go through this book again. Either way, it's okay! Your story, your relationship, and your glow are unique to you.

A way for you to remember the purpose of your glow—which you can carry throughout the book and, more purposefully, into your lives—is with this simple acronym:

- **G**ive to each other and the world with your unique mission and gifts.
- **L**ove one another with intention, emotion, and lots of deep breaths.
- **O**ffer grace and compassion to yourself and each other as you repair.
- **W**elcome in laughter, fun, and learning each day.

As you use this rubric, you can get your bearings. You will need some structure as you continue to be shaped and formed by your most meaningful relationships throughout your life. Your brain is organized in such a way that the neurons and their linking synapses actually need strategies and challenges to keep them firing. You achieve more neuroplasticity (change) as you lean in to do the work with as much positivity as you can wisely muster. Doing your relationship work encourages brain, body, and emotional health with all the new moves you are trying out.

Couples who challenge one another indeed grow stronger. And isn't that what we all want?

AFTERGLOW

Illuminate: What stage of the Enneagram Glow do you think you are in right now? Think about it or talk it out.

Spark Up Heart-to-Heart Conversation: Ask your spouse, "What do you think we could do to move through the glow stages to get to our 2.0 or afterglow?" If things get tense, don't be afraid to take a break, pause, and take some deep breaths.

Glow Brightly Together: Plan to use your gifts together to help someone else this week. Who will that be?

2

The Enneagram and Levels of Relationship Health in Marriage

Till this moment I never knew myself.

JANE AUSTEN[1]

It was my first actual paid job in the field of couples work. I was so wet behind the ears that when I said yes to the job, I didn't even realize it was in private practice. Yikes! That was a lot of responsibility to take on, but I was so happy to be hired as part of a group I believed in.

After grad school, Wes and I had moved back to Michigan to help my mother, who had suffered a stroke. My father was still teaching and needed some administrative help beyond what he and my other siblings were already doing. It was a lot to take on with a brand-new job, but I was confident I was up to the task.

As my couples practice grew to bustling and busy, I fully embraced the feel of city life, green tea frappuccinos on the go, and life in the fast lane. I thought that having as many social engagements as possible through the week was the only way to live, and Wes agreed. Our pace was dizzying to say the least, but the combination of caffeine and youthful idealism was a fragrant accompaniment to this swirling season.

In those youthful days when we are vacillating between being afraid and dauntless before more truly humbling life experiences ground us, there is often an accompaniment of arrogance. This was indeed one of those times. I'd already been through so much and done my own hard work in therapy (emphasis on "done"). I thought I had it covered.

As you can imagine, life's realities did eventually hit. Some of them were hard, and some were grand. Isn't that life? I became pregnant with our first child, Hannah, almost as soon as I started my job.

Needless to say, my stress levels went up after becoming a parent. I walked through transitions in my life and body that created changes in me forever but shrugged them all off as "no biggie." Instead of grieving my losses and seeing my body's war wounds as casualties of sorts, everything was "interesting" and "a science experiment" to me.

While on maternity leave, I took on an enormous project to lead the therapy team at work to business accreditation. I became a clinical director of sorts and worked every single second while my daughter was napping. When I wasn't working, I was kickboxing or doing chores. My days were planned with efficiency so my daughter could get the utmost ideal care when she was awake. Along with my siblings, I was also working to care for my mother, getting her to any medical appointments as needed.

These are humbling experiences to look back on a decade later. I remember the often futile attempts of walking both my mother and a toddler in a car seat to an appointment, only to have one or the other of them try to run off.

Not long after, our second child, Melody Jane, was born. Though life with our girls and growing family was beautiful, there were also plenty of hard times. Still, there was joy in the service. Life was brimming with possibility, even hope for Mom's healing with new medicines or therapies for a while.

A still deeper test of personality came on the fateful morning when that hope for healing was dashed. That day, my mother died suddenly. I was holding my third child, nine-month-old Jack, in one hand and a glass of water in the other when I got the call. Instinctively I dropped the glass and fell into a sadness that is hard to describe. I was functional but heartbroken. Once again, there was a shift in my emotional health.

What I've finally faced is that no amount of scholarship or all the mental planning a thinking type does can prepare us for shocks in life. There are inevitable losses along the route of life in marriage and family—the small ones that change us slowly and the big ones that change us interminably. Knowing what grief and pain were as constructs did not suffice for me. This knowledge only sharpened the gross disparity between theoretical living and my new reality. Although I was no longer arrogant or smug in this new reality, I still thought I could do it all. I still pushed forward. My maladaptive pattern under stress was locked into place: Just try to keep moving to survive.

Do you too remember a time when you departed from what seemed like your A game, even in a way that seemed unavoidable? Perhaps you went within yourself as a self-protective measure, or you achieved to the hilt and moved even faster. Maybe you stopped communicating with your spouse or you had an affair.

When stress hits, we try to control our situations with what has worked for us in the past. These strategies may have truly helped us in childhood, but now as adults, with the ability to fend for ourselves in more well-rounded and healthily adaptive ways, we find these old ways tend to hurt us and our relationships more than they help.

Since I still had all of the best research and relationship tools at my disposal as a marriage therapist, despite my high-stress levels from raising young children and caring for an ailing parent, I felt I was pretty much always right whenever Wes and I had a marriage discussion in that season. And though my work indeed kept us on track with the reminder for basic date nights and communication tools, my arrogance turned out to be one of the harder aspects of him being married to a therapist. Like everyone else's, my levels of relationship health swell and fall with the tides of life.

Relational arrogance is also a human issue, since most of us have the availability bias as an issue. We believe that we have reasons we act certain ways, so we are deserving of grace. We think our spouse messes up because they're not as intrinsically healthy as we are. In most of us, there is an unspoken statement that, although we ourselves can't help but act out in maladaptive, deeply rooted ways, our partner can and should do better with their hardships.

So even with all the great marriage tools at our disposal, the shadows still found Wes and me. I turned to fear, he turned to anger, and at times, we both turned to despair.

Up and down our relationship tides went. Since we nurtured our faith lives with God and got self-care, we often did okay. We used basic marriage tools like weekly date nights, which kept us barely (and I do mean barely) afloat. But we didn't find out how to work through our issues as a couple—to find our true 2.0 glow or afterglow seasons of marriage—until we learned about the Enneagram.

The Enneagram tips and tools we learned gently but firmly confirmed the things we had both been trying to say about one another for years. It was the gentle but direct confrontation we needed. *You are stuck in your negative coping strategies, and here's how. You have a reason you are here, and these strategies were once helpful to you. But they are no longer helping you. In fact, they may be killing your relationship.*

Suddenly, I was tuned in to how arrogant I had been about my vantage point. Many of my personality qualities that had formerly been my pride and joy were pieces of myself that hurt others. Now I was embarrassed. This is often the initial response for someone who finds out more about their Enneagram type and is hit with the hardest aspects of it. This may sound familiar to you also.

Wes had a very strong reaction when he discovered his type. In fact, he physically pushed the computer away before muttering, "I'm a perfectionist." It took him a solid read of the neat type One checklist in Ian Morgan Cron and Suzanne Stabile's *The Road Back to You* before the Enneagram discovery of his type crystallized.[2] As a type One, he was so impressed with the neatness, efficiency, and order of the checklists in each chapter that he was actually quite happy, truth be told.

As you consider your own individual and relationship journey toward health and healing, my first hope is that you'll be ready to face your issues here in these pages with me. My next hope is that you'll avoid future years of denial of your own issues. No one else can do or validate this work for you. This is your journey, and you know yourself better than anyone else.

This was true for Wes and me too. In fact, since we were both such ambitious, functional people in our jobs and church life before we did our Enneagram work, we were praised and reinforced by all who knew us. They saw the maladaptive, busy, spinning patterns and thought we were some sort of acrobatic superheroes, not realizing our loving and serving the world were costing us our very relationship health. The knowledge we gained in learning about ourselves through the Enneagram helped us out of that challenging season. My hope is that the same will be true for you too.

Your Turn to Learn

Now it's your turn to learn about the best and worst of your type. Here, you're going to learn what your personality type typically looks like in life and relationships, whether in healthy seasons, stressed seasons, or times of dysfunction. Consider these hallmarks as guideposts to help you identify levels of health and opportunities for insight and growth in your type.

In a moment, we'll take a deeper look at your types. Because the traits here are described in terms of health, stress, and dysfunction, *be aware that if you and/or your spouse are in healthy places right now, many of the more stressful trait issues won't apply and may never apply.* However, if you do find yourself in a state of stress or dysfunction, you'll be able to use the steps and the traits of your type in relational health for cues.

Whatever their type, someone in a severely dysfunctional state will need ongoing care in a variety of ways, including mental, physical, emotional, and spiritual self-care, as well as intentional couples work if they are in a relationship.

Sometimes the healthy traits take a long time to find, and more often they ebb and flow in our lives. Since typically our gifts as well as the dysfunctional patterns in our typology started from our very earliest gifts and defense mechanisms of childhood, we need to give growth time to settle in.

Though I had few problems in my early days, the humbling process of both my life's losses and doing my Enneagram and marriage work has made me a much deeper, stronger person, as well as a more gracious marriage helper and spouse. My hope is that discovering more about your type—in the healthy, stressful, and dysfunctional seasons of life—will help you do the same.

Let's do our work with a deep breath, with hope for figuring things out, and with a long-game approach about how we glow together best as we take a deeper dive into each of our types.

Type One Levels of Relationship Health

A One in Relational Health

A healthy One in marriage is kind, is orderly, and responsibly takes time in self-care and partner care. They healthily release the resentment and anger that build up in their body. Instead of being rigid, they consider that there are multiple perspectives and that their view is not the only angle. They realize that individuals of varying personality types (including their spouse) have unique gifts and challenges, and thus they withhold negative judgment about others. They color in their own often linear analysis with this analytical view as well as compassionate care. Instead of always responding to their guttural reactions, they can pause and take a few deep breaths when they get overwhelmed. They can bring logic, positivity, lightness, and emotional closeness in conflict rather than coldness, resentment, or distancing. Theoretically, they are not simply idealists but are also thoughtful, pragmatic, relational spouses and people, considerate of their spouse's views and not punitive in any way. Their gut instincts are balanced with their caring hearts, and their thinking is not overly inhibited by their inner critic.

A One can reason, plan, bring order, and show fairness, largely gracious in their assessment of the way things should go in their marriages and families as they trust all brokenness to God. They are open to gratefully seeing the gift of what is already in their beloved life, imperfections and all. They offer softness and relaxation to their people after they've released stress and let in balance. As they unburden themselves, they exhibit great joy in life—perhaps more joy than any other type when they're in this balance—and they take regular vacations and mini retreats to keep a healthy work-life balance.

In terms of helping their partner to shine or glow, Ones often open their spouse to realize that they are capable of hard work and goodness in ways they never thought possible.

A One in Relational Stress

A moderately distressed One in marriage may struggle with perfectionism. They may even pride themselves on being perfect or on their expectations for the perfection of others. In doing so, they may frequently demand that others do their bidding in a way they deem right (which is generally perfect in the way they see it). They will pursue this on a regular basis even if it almost kills them. They may sacrifice self-care, rest, or quality time alone and with their spouse—usually all of it on any given day when the work is not done.

They may be zealous or self-punitive or use their defense mechanism of reaction formation to indulge in socially and culturally inappropriate practices, deeming that the imperfection of others has earned them the right to be divergent from their typically exceedingly high moral standards. If they have a strong feeling that they are right, they may also believe that rage, disguised as righteous anger, is an appropriate response.

This stage is marked by busyness, high stress levels, and little healthy return for their investment. In this way, they often burn out on this kind of living by about age thirty, with a health crisis or a divorce in many cases. At this point, they learn to soften or find healthy routes, such as a weekly massage, a daily workout, an over-the-counter mood stabilizer, or perhaps an SSRI medication from their doctor to help keep them more positive. They may, however, find enough stability and release nonmedically with regular fitness, a rich spiritual life, and emotional routines that they commit to. A daily gratitude practice may help, as well as loving their spouse even if they feel regularly irritated by them. As stress cannot be helped, a One in this stage may also add habit-tracking cues and systems for getting out in nature, take occasional vacations, and have date nights, which will help their spouse to see that there are still elements of fun and softness in them when they are finally relaxed and have released stress.

As a One gets healthier and faces their shadows, they often become more grateful for the help they are given, even when it is not done to their standards. As they reward their spouse with loving gestures for their efforts, the couple can better work toward their goals together. Likewise, the more a spouse is critiqued by the One, the less likely they are to work toward their goals.

A One in Relational Dysfunction

A One in a highly dysfunctional state in marriage will have frequent anger, resentment, and fits of jealousy and be very reactive. They may have major health issues and visit the doctor frequently, experiencing somatic complaints because of personal bodily neglect as they strive for perfection due to their incessant and relentless inner critic. They may often shoot verbal darts at those closest to them and at themselves instead of allowing in grace and serenity.

They are also often engaged in backdoor behaviors, such as alcohol abuse or other addictions. Some even begin affairs. They may justify these behaviors by rationalizing that they had to find an outlet for their righteous anger. Ones may also have an eating disorder, a personality disorder, obsessive-compulsive disorder, a depressive disorder, or anxiety, depending on their instinctual variant.

If You Love a One

If you love a One, remember that their biggest desire is to make the world a better place with their improver gifts. This is not only their desire, it is their gift. You too will be on the road to improvement if you chose to partner with a One. Sometimes that's even unconsciously why you picked them, as you knew they would keep you on the straight and narrow. Try to remember that when your One is trying to reform you, it's because they care. However, if it's within your reach, steer them to fun, art, bodywork, and thinking about other things besides further improvements.

Remember that you cannot be perfect for them, but remind them that you will always seek excellence in your personality type and gifting. You simply have a different gifting than they do. Help them to understand how to frame things more positively, and realize that their very gifting for seeing errors makes this hard for them.

Type Two Levels of Relationship Health

A Two in Relational Health

A healthy Two in marriage is caring and considerate, helping their spouse and others without completely sacrificing their own self-care, self-knowledge, and moral integrity. They set aside daily time for thinking and some type of health and spiritual practice, usually before the busy day unfolds. They understand that if they don't incorporate these things, they won't do well in life or in marriage. Refreshed, they come at life without manipulation and as naturally lavish givers, truly enjoying sharing and helping their beloved partner. They also speak up when their needs are not met in a partnership, whether emotionally, sexually, financially, or otherwise.

A thriving Two cares deeply about those in their family and has no reason to try to charm or manipulate them or others outside the home. They do not see themselves as more important than their children because they have enough self-esteem from their own self-care and hard work in their marriage. They likewise do not see their children as above them or others or as perfect little angels. Instead, they know their children are beloved, growing individuals in process like everyone else. They see every single person as equally loved and deserving of praise.

Though a Two loves to regularly reach out to help and spend time with others, they understand boundaries are important for a job well done. They say no to many outside giving projects and people when their own self-care, marriage care, family care, or rest is at stake. They also seek God to replenish them instead of expecting only others to do so, and they drink in the knowledge that they are beloved by their Creator even while at rest or without the perfect mood all the time. They know that emotions of all kinds are necessary and that, just as there is a time for fun and giving, there is also a time for resting alone and with family.

In terms of helping their partner to shine or glow, Twos often help their spouse to feel adored, well nurtured, and fulfilled by their sacrificial love in ways their partner never thought possible. They also remind their spouse of the sheer pleasure that can be found in giving wholeheartedly to others.

A Two in Relational Stress

A moderately distressed Two in marriage is frantic and frazzled. They are tired of doing everything for the family and feeling like they don't get much in return. Thus, they latch on to others in the community to get their perceived and neglected needs for affirmation and sustenance met. They are tired of feeling like their spouse doesn't care about them above others. They can be intense when it comes to fighting for their needs to be met, and they can get very pushy and even manipulative when others—including their spouse and children—set boundaries, as they manipulate or demand that they get their needs recompensed for their labor.

A Two may also flirt with others to manipulate their spouse into giving them more attention instead of directly and maturely asking for it. This is not always because they especially like the third party but so that they may deal with issues of neglect and trauma, and they attempt to find their worth in another. They may use illness, sexual appeal, or eating and control issues to try to usurp their spouse's attention or the attention of other power figures in the extended family rather than asking for it directly and with firm boundaries. They may also say yes to everything in the community to get more love and attention. That creates a hard dynamic in their marriage, as needs cannot easily be met on either side at least partly because of a lack of the Two's emotional presence, even while they're at home.

A Two in Relational Dysfunction

A Two in a highly dysfunctional state in marriage is in most cases suffering from a lack of healthy body care or a lack of healthy emotional scanning. They may even be having an emotional or physical affair with multiple partners out of the histrionic desire to get love and attention from an unquenchable source. They may be addicted to a substance like alcohol, Adderall, other uppers, or pills of some sort that promise to allow them to carry on relationships with their children or spouse to any healthy degree.

In many cases, there is an unaddressed memory of an abuse suffered in the past, often physical, emotional, or sexual abuse or neglect. Here, a Two isn't in process to change the cycle but may be perpetuating it in some way. Their vice of pride and hedonistic desires creates a pattern of avoiding the humility it takes to admit that, as much as they long to help, they too need help to get well.

If You Love a Two

If you love a Two, encourage them to use their thought life to guide them daily and to let God lead them to what is theirs to do so they don't overbook or let their feelings exclusively guide them. Remind them to revisit the past for cues and look to the future for plans, not just perseverate on relationships right now. When they ask for validation, try to give it, but don't nurse any unhealthy pride. Let them know you love that they are doing their best and you understand their insecurity but that you want to validate their beloved worth.

Remember their biggest need with you is nurture of the relationship and your participation in that nurturing. Know that when they manipulate to get someone to give back to them, it isn't out of cruelty. Instead, it's coming from a desire to genuinely find love. Encourage your Two in their love language (not just yours!). Try to help them feel safe by regularly depositing love tokens and assuring them that they are first in your heart, especially if you are someone who does not show that outwardly all the time.

Type Three Levels of Relationship Health

A Three in Relational Health

A healthy Three in marriage is able to focus on not just their glorious work and destiny for greatness but also their beloved partner and family with the same zeal and high ethic. They're generally able to put work down during certain designated hours and to stay attuned and present with their families even if they have to get creative to settle down. In this way, they seek and find routes to relaxation. They take time to learn about their deeper worth outside of work and the importance of boundaries. They are diplomatic truth tellers but also some of the most caring and generous souls on the planet.

The healthy Three also gets daily self-care and is in the process of finding who they are outside of just their performance statistics or curriculum vitae. They have stable traits across a number of environments and rarely deceive themselves or others. A Three may love systematic family flowcharts as well as have extremely high standards. They often hold family meetings but also try to add in encouragement, fun, softness, and grace, even taking time alone to think and process before being harsh. In this way they are well-connected with their emotions and know how to ask directly for love versus demand it via control or manipulation. They understand that when their spouse complains about them, taking a deep breath, pausing, and remembering their worth outside of perfection are healthy. They are allowed to make mistakes, and they know it. Therefore, they create intentional shifts toward honesty in every conversation. They too can be open about needs and directly ask for those needs in marriage to be met by their partner.

A healthy Three can be strong yet apologetic as needed. They prioritize their family with their whole heart rather than just chasing the next success. They love their partner not just as "arm candy" or somebody beautiful or accomplished near them. Instead, they truly understand that their partner's beloved worth is from God. Their spouse is a gift, and their entire family has special gifts that should be cherished, shared, and celebrated, not merely displayed for gain.

In terms of helping their partner to shine or glow, Threes often help their spouse to realize their gifts and voice and to manage their gifts with success and excellence in order to accomplish something truly beautiful.

A Three in Relational Stress

A moderately distressed Three in marriage needs to be the center of attention. This is often due to being overly coddled or severely neglected in the past. This Three likely feels the need to work at all times, both vocationally and relationally. Instead of settling into closeness and comfort, they work *on* the marriage versus being *in* the marriage. They settle for being loved for their achievements instead of who they are because they don't actually know who they are, or at least not very well. When things get difficult at home, then, they simply end up working harder to impress their spouse. Working also reduces the anxiety they feel and helps those in the workplace and at home to think they are on top of it all.

This admittance of underlying anxiety is terrifying at first to a moderately distressed Three, but it's an important space for them to troubleshoot. When they stop long enough to address a troubled underlying spirit, they can come back to self-care, self-maintenance, and the self-agency that goes beneath the surface. They can begin to access their true and inherent worth.

However, many moderately dysfunctional Threes will not make this trek. This is when a married Three can move into deceit and start to engage in addictive behavior. They feel they need others to support their identity so they can ride on the coattails of those seemingly stronger and more secure people who have validated their worth. Since they can easily camouflage to meet the needs of others, finding someone to ride this wave with them is not difficult, though it will also not satiate. Ironically, the other party is often just as stressed or dysfunctional as they too walk this backdoor route to getting their deepest needs for love met in the shadows.

A Three in Relational Dysfunction

A dysfunctional Three in marriage is likely completely addicted to work, finding accolades at work dinners or via social media while also climbing the social, sexual, or material ladder of success. This ladder leads to the dark alleys of sexual addiction, nothingness, deeper anxiety, and deep feelings of shame. This powerful facade is just that—a facade—and far from the healthy space of peace and true restfulness that a Three deeply needs. Their insufferable conquering leads them down the path of narcissistic selfishness, and they don't let anyone stop them from getting what they want to the exact measure they want it.

At this level, a Three is codependent but often doesn't have much of a moral compass or relationship with God. Unless they snap out of it, they won't have much pity for anybody who's blocking them. This is an important place for the Three to get therapy or strong, well-boundaried pastoral help so that they can deal with deeper underlying issues and learn how to parse out relationships. They need to find safe and healthy relationships that are not just about work or goal getting but that are loving and comforting, which is what their marriage can potentially become. They should strive to engage these goals with maturity, vulnerability, and imperfection. At the end of the day, the heart-oriented Three still truly wants a relationship to thrive, but they may go about dastardly ways to get there.

If You Love a Three

If you love a Three, remember that though they show a rather tough facade, they desire a very close and loyal bond. Most of the time, Threes have had an overabundance or underabundance of nurture, perhaps both across time. In either case, they feel best when they know where their spouse is at all times and when their spouse is highly attuned to their sensitive hearts. Remember that they won't be honest with you unless you're willing to stay and work things out with them, since their shadow side is deceit and they desperately want your love and approval. They won't tell or even necessarily know what they feel unless they are confident that you won't leave them, which is their worst fear. Apart from their romantic relationships, they do an amazing job of speaking the truth in love, and a Three loves when you appreciate them both inside and outside of their work ethic.

Remind them that you too will move in closer when they are softer and learn to speak the truth in love. Encourage them to apologize after being harsh, even if it takes a while. Let them know how attractive it is to you when they take care of themselves and discover who they really are. Encourage them in self-care, and remember they need to feel safe before they can release the truth. This is not your fault. At some point in their earlier lives or in previous generations, the truth was *not* safe, so they want to make sure they have that safety with you.

Type Four Levels of Relationship Health

A Four in Relational Health

A healthy Four in marriage is creative and loves relating with their partner and family in terms of ideals. They dream, but their daydreams do not take over. They are not so idealistic that they need to have a perfect marriage or a "stars align" kind of emotional and sexual intimacy every time they connect with their spouse. Instead, a healthy Four can embrace the messy parts of life, including themselves, with grace. They can see themselves and others without self-hatred or partner hatred, without ranking themselves as above or below others, and with a winsome delight versus animosity.

In marriage, a Four at their best is endearing, gentle, creative, and compassionate. A Four is mindful to take slow steps as they express themselves naturally and to ensure they have something valuable to contribute when they do approach others. Since they are so careful and deep and see the world in creative, vivid gradients, they need to be given time to process and move in all areas of life.

A Four knows how to bring hope, beauty, and human connection even out of their painful moments and helps their families and spouse to do the same. They deeply care about the needs of their spouse and maintain ideals about them. They know that envy and melancholy may threaten to swoop in and take them down, but they give proper time for these expressions, moving from lament into gratitude and activity. A Four in health has a light and fun side, full of joy and wonder that is enchanting to behold. They truly mesmerize and captivate others with their way of displaying beauty and wonder.

In terms of helping their partner to shine or glow, Fours often help their spouse to realize that despite their broken pieces, they are worthy, accepted, and dazzling just as they are.

A Four in Relational Stress

A moderately distressed Four in marriage has good moments but is often stuck in a victim mentality, enviously wondering if they drew the short end of the straw when it comes to receiving love. They compare their lives and their marriages to the best of what they see in extended family members and friends, as well as those on social media, and often rank themselves as more downtrodden in comparison.

They will also often rank their spouse as either above or below others, forgetting their spouse too is beloved simply because they are human. If they rank their spouse highly, they may revere them, but if they are having an off moment, they may cast them away because their spouse doesn't meet all their nuanced ideals. These expressions and comparisons may even coincide or follow very quickly one after another, which keeps them in a push-pull relationship with their bewildered spouse. Their lack of reliability, their withdrawal, and other times their raw, needy, and vulnerable emotions send mixed signals.

The Four's spouse and others may see them as snobbish and feel unable to meet their high, idealistic standards. Internally the Four propels such habits to cover the shame that accompanies ranking themselves as lower than others. They feel that they need somebody to understand them, pander to their changing fields of vision, and bring them up. In this conundrum, they can fixate on one person—spouse or otherwise—who is out of reach idealistically. A dysfunctional Four may talk themselves out of relationship success altogether even with a sincere and caring spouse. In this posture they can sabotage themselves by creating a self-fulfilling prophecy of rejection in their marriage.

They may become addicted in attempts to handle the darkness they feel inside, especially if they don't get bodywork in daily life, such as fitness, dance, meditation, or artistic outlets. Bodily stress release is critical for a Four, who frequently feels they have too much to bear and spends an excessive amount of time in contemplative thought. They may otherwise disappear into a hobby or a fantasy life many hours a day, disengaging from their marriage.

A Four in Relational Dysfunction

A dysfunctional Four in marriage not only goes into unpredictable withdrawal but can become highly manipulative with reactive, critical rages against their spouse, their children, and at times themselves. They may engage in self-harm or other destructive behaviors. They are emotionally unstable and likely have a co-occurring mood disorder or addiction issue.

This Four is skeptical that others can ever understand their complexity, so they must drown out their sorrows in some panacea. If an addiction begins, they end up self-sabotaging the work others try to do with them for recovery and spiral back into victimhood. If their partner is one of the people they alternately idolize and castigate, the Four will likely stay with them even if the pairing is terribly dysfunctional unless they have found another healthy person to meet their ideals, which is unlikely in this state. The Four will alternately accept and deliver the very worst.

If You Love a Four

If you love a Four, remember that when they feel uncertain about your relationship, they will test you to see if you love them.

They want to see an emotional reaction from you as they wonder whether you love them or are willing to give them a very precious commodity: your time. A Four also needs plenty of time to withdraw individually so they can take breaks from their compassion and busy days. This time alone often helps them to understand themselves better, so you can encourage them to find gratitude in those moments. Since they are idealists and romantics, they appreciate you making even small and seemingly insignificant moments special, such as when you arrive or depart. Even if you have only a few moments together, they can be quality and special ones.

Remember that a Four doesn't evoke emotions from you to be cruel but because they are feeling lonely and rejected. Don't abandon them here, but encourage them to find time with God, to do their bodywork, and to find space while also assuring them of your love.

Type Five Levels of Relationship Health

A Five in Relational Health

A healthy Five in marriage uses their tremendously focused analytical gifting and specialized brain power to help their family and community in a practical, efficient manner. The relationally healthy Five knows how to move from work systems to their family system, even if it takes a transition to pry their minds from their intensely focused projects. They know that after synthesis of information, they need to move into a healthy progression of engaging and sharing themselves with their spouse and family. This Five is not only logical but also able to express emotion as needed, even if their feelings are thought more than felt. They can find positivity and rhythms of hope instead of being rationalistically nihilistic. Though a Five is often introverted in many senses, they are also deeply relational at their best, opening their hearts to care about those hurting, whatever the cost.

A healthy Five brings good systems of maintenance to the family because of their well-researched planning and quest for the best life hacks. Their spouse knows that they like to play, tease, hide away in research, and banter back and forth. However, when it comes to the big moments, they are there for them more than for any other person. While they may be impish and playful, using wit and dark humor, a Five is deeply caring, honorable, and sensitive to the most pressing needs of their spouse.

In terms of helping their partner to shine or glow, Fives often anchor their spouse, helping them to realize that they are capable of putting time and focus into their dreams. They slow them down to savor the wonder of the natural earth and the delicacies of life and to fathom other innovative discoveries.

A Five in Relational Stress

A moderately distressed Five in marriage is distracted and gets scattered in their efforts to save and manage their resources. Instead of working out their internal struggle of competency with their spouse directly, they may take a back route to solving issues, such as delving into risky behaviors obsessively. They don't do these things to act out but to escape the gnawing sense of inadequacy. Sometimes they don't participate in risky behaviors at all, leaving them in the fantasy zone. Either way, these diversions take much emotional and tactical space, so it's important that the Five discontinues negative coping strategies and talks to their spouse directly about what's really bothering them. They also do very well with structured couples counseling or coaching work.

The hope for a Five at this level is that they find they do not *have* to know everything in order to be quite competent. In marriage, it's important for them to learn that their self-esteem is not dependent on their spouse's admiration—or anyone's, for that matter—but this does not give them license to retreat from relationships. Instead, staying strong with presence and power as well as kindness and an ability to compromise will help most Fives. Though they worry endlessly over running out of resources, they find that when they engage with their spouse and community, they will always have enough, even though they also know they need their precious boundaries, rest, and privacy.

In stress, a Five likely feels powerless at work or is otherwise unable to say no to projects, which can infuriate their spouse, who now sees even less of them. The Five needs to take some deep breaths and be kind but speak out. They also need to continue to set boundaries and take breaks from their multiple-brain-tabs-open context switching at work, something they do in their fixation of gathering resources. They may also need a holistic anxiety supplement, if not psychopharmacological care, from a reliable medical provider. A Five in distress often struggles with trusting the competency of doctors, so finding a professional they trust for a wellness path is a major win.

Many Fives love YouTube or books as trusted sources. Working out physically also helps them tremendously on a daily basis. A Five thrives in team sports as well as individual sports as long as they have a predictable, regimented schedule. If they decide to participate in activities, they greatly enjoy their time in playful competition with themselves or others. Their spouse often enjoys supporting them in this space that fuels their competency and fitness.

When they find a predictable pace, Fives can let go of other mental fixations and focus on their families and careers with more presence and confidence. They begin to embrace their inner strength and energy reserves as well as their lighter, playful stance with less scattering and less glut of information.

A Five in Relational Dysfunction

A dysfunctional Five in marriage is entrenched in knowledge seeking, potentially in conspiracy theories, and in paranoia. It's even possible they experience some form of psychosis. They are semi-aware of it but can't easily find their way out of the rabbit hole once they are down it. Sometimes they have leaned so far to the left or to the right politically that they feel they can trust almost no one outside of their tiny sphere of influence. They are quickly moving away from the relational zone, and it seems they can never go quite deep enough in the quest for more information. Thus, they end up isolating themselves even more from others. They may begin to question if God is punishing them for various small nuances that no one else can answer or explain to their satisfaction. They become so deeply invested in theories or ideas about their current fascinations and obsessions that their spouse gets almost nothing from them.

This is a time when their spouse may rightly threaten to leave because they may feel the Five has no time and energy for them. Then the Five must decide to lean in or out of life and family. They may vacillate between rage at themselves or their spouse and terror or guilt. Their sleeping and thinking may become even more fragmented, their thoughts more self-judging, and their participation in life erratic. They may become addicted to alcohol or psychedelic experiences.

If You Love a Five

If you love a Five, remember it takes them a few days to process emotions, so they often can't just speak to your emotional questions or concerns right away. However, they can learn to listen and have compassion for you even if their experience is different. Try to remind them of this so they're not left bewildered in this terrifying realm. They also may not want or even need

71

the same level of socializing as you. Still, their love delves deep, and they may offer the little time they feel they have to you and other loved ones in potentially unseen but significant ways. It's important to remember that in most cases, you fell in love with the Five for their focus and stability, so enjoy those gifts instead of wishing for others. Don't demand what they can't give. They love helping in ways they can, as they are relational even though often introverted.

In the withdrawing stance and with their past-focused lens, the Five historically has been disappointed. If they share any part of their interests or story with you, honor it. Try to get them into their body and find healthy ways to transition from research, reminding them that there is always more to discover. That synergy with you will bring them more energy for the many discoveries ahead.

Type Six Levels of Relationship Health

A Six in Relational Health

A healthy Six in marriage knows how to relax and have fun in their marriage as well as how to plan. They also know how to step into courage and action even when they're stuck in fear, so they usually take on some form of movement or bodywork versus getting locked inside their busy or spiraling minds. They greatly enjoy helping their spouses and family members to troubleshoot issues, and they can laugh about their neurotic tendencies. They are not depressed and anxious about their very real issues but hold out practical hope and take active steps to heal. They have learned to trust themselves and many in their community of support, who can aid them when they get stuck in decision-making.

When their spouse is angry or upset with them, a Six is able to resist controlling or excessive reactivity, taking time to think about things and find the silver lining. With this intrinsic pausing, they need time to think and patiently discuss the issues at hand. Deep breaths and healthy distractions also keep them from having a tantrum, and this raises their self-efficacy, or the belief that they can do hard things. In this posture, they learn and grow while being remarkably patient as they wait for their spouse to do the same. They're not tempted to try to take all matters into their own hands or to project their insecurities and distrust onto their spouse. Because they are verbal processors in most cases, they love to talk to their spouse about problems. However, they can read nonverbal cues so their spouse can let them know when they are overwhelmed and are done talking. If the Six has more to say, verbal processing can continue alone or with a trusted friend.

Sometimes a Six requests help and fixing, and other times they just want a shoulder to cry on. No matter what, they need to get active fitness and self-care, release their worries in faith, and take time for lighthearted fun. All of this must be routinely planned, as this self-care is not intuitive for many youthful Sixes. They may or may not also take an over-the-counter stress medication or an SSRI or other anxiety medication to manage their reactivity and anxiety. A healthy Six knows how to ask for professional help as well as how to take initiative. They work to get enough sleep at night, to take mental pauses, and to share their caring heart with their spouse and others.

In terms of helping their partner to shine or glow, Sixes often help their spouse take their time to plan well, reminding them that they are beloved and deserving of protection and support no matter what. Sixes also love when their spouse shows strong leadership skills and will praise and encourage leadership in them. This praise feels great to the spouse because it comes from such an intelligent source.

A Six in Relational Stress

A moderately distressed Six in marriage is highly anxious, and that can lead to them becoming overly controlling and paranoid or even reaching out to someone besides their spouse for security. This is especially true if they feel that their spouse has disappointed them or abandoned them in some way, whether it be financially, physically, emotionally, or in multiple ways. A moderately unhealthy Six also may have a difficult time taking responsibility for hurting a spouse, and they may rush into verbal and emotional defense before taking a pause. In many cases, they may *want* to let their spouse off the hook for past offenses but feel afraid that by doing so the pattern will repeat, so they try to control their spouse in some ways. They may state that they will never be able to trust them again, holding their marital vows over their partner while the spouse is forced to make an eternal penance.

When stressed, a Six may also go into a withdrawing, slothful state, seeking wisdom from perceived authority figures so much that they don't depend on themselves at all for solving problems. From this vantage point, either they lean too hard on a spouse if the spouse is one of their mentors, or they lean too far away. The marriage can begin to unravel because of too much dependency at times and too much withdrawing into seemingly safe corners at other times.

If Sixes are able to get fitness every day with a soothing and at least somewhat arousing or intense routine, their anxiety substantially subsides. A moderately distressed Six knows which medications help them and which doctors do not take advantage of their sensitive, impressionable natures so they can get help in times of need. Spiritual care and breathing exercises are of utmost importance for a Six, who needs to step from fear to courage, as is letting God deal with their plans after they've done a reasonable amount of planning. When they can release control, lean into compromise with their spouse or family, and talk things out a little more calmly and directly with pauses as needed, they are back on the safe track.

A Six in Relational Dysfunction

A dysfunctional Six in marriage has been anxiously aroused or paranoid for so long that they start to become severely anxious. At this point, panic sets in, and they may temporarily need strong medications or other daily self-soothing methods to calm themselves down. They may procrastinate and avoid taking responsibility due to depression and anxiety, while also trying to take comfort in political or religious missions. They may even become violently attuned to a neurotic or fear-mongering leader of some sort.

Their spouse may sense that they are so out of control that they can no longer understand reality. The Six may even become so fearful that they cannot leave the home. Yet they persist in their delusions or paranoia—often in both. They may rage at their spouse, who does not agree with them on all these fronts with the same reactive passion.

Their spouse may leave them when the paranoia becomes too great or the Six becomes violent. Alternatively, their spouse may insist they get inpatient or outpatient treatment for mental health issues, such as dialectical behavioral therapy for bipolar or their paranoia.

If You Love a Six

If you love a Six, remember that they are often at a loss for a trusted sense of self in the relationship, and they need reassurance from you that they are on the right track. Often something in their past made them feel they were not safe on their own. Because they hold so much wisdom, they sometimes feel very old and at other times very young. It's hard for them to find a middle ground with all their floating thoughts and concerns, so validating their healthy thoughts and findings and using some of their best ideas is key to helping them back to confidence and an interchange of healthy self-respect and partner respect.

Encourage them to set a time limit to deliberate their issues versus running your schedule with every worry that pops into their heads. This means you will need to set boundaries since they will likely push, but gently encourage them back into their virtue of courage as many times as needed. This may be as simple as reminding them to take some time on their own to verbally process uncomfortable issues. Also encourage fitness to make sure they're letting off mental steam. If they have a faith life, help them to spend time writing or speaking in prayerful gratitude.

Type Seven Levels of Relationship Health

A Seven in Relational Health

A healthy Seven in marriage is full of joy, enthralled with the small sweetnesses in life, and interpersonally engaged in their marriage and family. They know how to balance their desire for wonder and pleasant extroverted experiences with focused work and healthy emotional and body expression. They understand that their spouse has gifts to give them that are different from their own and do not see themselves in a superior position or in an inferior joking or jesting position. Being a level-headed, trustworthy teammate to their spouse allows the Seven to find purposes beyond mere charm and to truly deliver depth to those they inspire.

This Seven understands that life has ups and downs as well as boring and painful moments. Thus, they can handle the bad days as well as the good, pausing, reflecting, and reframing in healthy ways instead of rationalizing everything negative away. Although emotions aren't always easy to handle, the healthy Seven knows that they can breathe deeply through the discomfort. They know how to process their emotions regularly, so they take time in this posture to slow down and allow life to be healthily analyzed and even felt with the body and heart. Their self-care is moderate versus extreme or absent. A healthy Seven enjoys pleasures but is able to savor them in the moment rather than anxiously looking for the next thing. When they are able to self-soothe and allow boredom or sadness to arise, they truly embrace the awe of life as well as the sorrows without constant stimulation, arousal, and hedonism.

The healthy Seven in marriage not only is focused on caring for their own needs but is encouraging, optimistic, innovative, patient, and joyful toward their spouse and family. They bring fun to the marriage and family with a creative and analytical mind, inviting others into holy play and holy rest.

In terms of helping their partner to shine or glow, Sevens often help their spouse to realize their potential with their encouragement and enthusiasm. They can remind them that anything is possible, encourage them to remember that they are beloved and gifted, and help them find joy and wonder in the simplest, smallest moments.

A Seven in Relational Stress

A moderately distressed Seven in marriage is constantly swirling in busyness, possibly from saying yes to everything. This is not all done just for the winning of pleasure but to avoid pain in others and themselves. In order not to hurt others' feelings, to manage precarious resources, or to avoid their uncomfortable deeper emotions, they say yes, yes, and more yes to the busy tasks asked of them. They may rationalize that they can get out of anything that's troubling them by staying as busy and resourceful as possible. In doing so, however, they may rob themselves of any real success because of this endless planning for pleasure.

Their gluttony for experience is a result of their untreated deeper anxiety. Unless it's faced, overdoing will stop them from doing anything that takes commitment and valor. Their spouse typically becomes upset with their frequent flying around to avoid feelings, leading the Seven into even more of a whirlwind as they also dodge their spouse's moods. The stressed Seven thinks that if they don't slow down, they may eventually catch up with this blurred, inconstant vision they are chasing. They don't realize their anxiety will be an Achilles' heel forever, lashing out at them for attention at an unforgiving pace.

This constant moving may also lead a Seven toward an addiction to pain pills or drugs of some sort. Instead of facing the grief and sadness that are important parts of life, they may develop bipolar or cyclothymia.

A Seven in Relational Dysfunction

A dysfunctional Seven in marriage is blinded by their busyness and activity, robbing their marriage of any semblance of intimacy and presence. They may desire harmony and convince themselves and their spouse that everything is okay even when the world is crashing down around them. They may not do this intentionally, but because they're moving so fast, they glibly believe everything is well. They instead press harder into their self-protectiveness and gluttony, refusing to face the sadness, menial tasks, and endings that are part of life.

In this activity level, a Seven's flights can range from moderately frenetic to a full-out manic-depressive type of state. Their emotions finally do catch up with them when they've bankrupted all resources, and these feelings come crashing down on top of them, often in heavy, physically exhausting ways. Then they may depressively isolate themselves, becoming obsessed with gaining security, researching ideas, or harboring fantasies. When they emerge from their isolation, they may once again become so busy with family and social events that they eventually collapse and repeat the vicious cycle. They may also deal with addiction or a sexual acting out of some sort.

In addition to addressing therapy with a twelve-step group, this Seven may need anxiety medication or mood stabilizers and would benefit from marital and individual therapy.

If You Love a Seven

If you love a Seven, help them learn to trust you. You can do this by using positive affirmation as much as possible, even to get them into emotions, rest, and disciplined practices. Instead of praising accomplishments, encourage them when you see them resting and focused. Celebrate when you see them partaking in any moderate activity. Give a gentle reminder that attending to emotional pain will not kill them but will actually bring them a more vibrant life. Share your needs, and sandwich critiques with praise. Remember to be gentle. You do not have to parent them. Allow life to teach them sometimes and step out of the way, but be ready to walk hand-in-hand with them as they mature and settle into trust with you.

Remember that they are anxious, and though it may seem as though their joy never has a landing place, it does. Therefore, it's very helpful for them to have a safe place to process feelings verbally—with God, a counselor, or even you in small doses, which they will love deep down. Sevens love to share joy and process with people, but they don't always know how to settle down and stay open to those emotions. Encourage them when you see those things happening, even briefly, as you shape new rhythms together.

Type Eight Levels of Relationship Health

An Eight in Relational Health

A healthy Eight in marriage has strength, drive, and energy for their spouse and children as well as their social causes and other big dreams. A healthy Eight is strong and fun but not dominating over their families. Instead of always leading, they enjoy simply taking part in the family. They understand that being with their spouse and family involves slowing down, listening, and letting the others generate opinions, ideas, and energy. There's a celebration, pride, and protection of their people, even though those people are different, as their ideas and gifts go out into the world. There is a deep loyalty between an Eight and their spouse and community. Though they have great energy, they have an ability to acknowledge it and harness it as needed, not overtaking situations or people.

A healthy Eight is not afraid of displaying the polarity of being both nurturing and strong in marriage. They are interesting and confident in their position as a spouse—the faithful partner of one person. They are patient with processes and are not likely to run away into another relationship or to run away from conflict. Instead, they will pause when they feel strong or defensive feelings arise inside of them, talk about the conflict in an organized and direct fashion, resolve it, work hard at staying in the relationship, and move on from issues without holding a grudge as long as they feel there has been resolution. They are tuned in to their bodies and self-care practices, knowing they may need even two workouts a day in order to get rid of their excess energy. However, they are not likely to overdo and exhaust themselves since they know how to rest and retreat by doing their favorite hobbies and research each day.

The Eight is not shy about their needs, but they are also eager to meet the needs of their spouse. They will help their spouse to feel value and power that no one else has ever given them.

In terms of helping their partner to shine or glow, Eights often help their spouse to realize that they are worthy of dignity, respect, and protection as well as loyalty and deep, nurturing love from their partner. They will help their partner to seek this kind of respect in the world as well.

An Eight in Relational Stress

A moderately distressed Eight in marriage keeps themselves busy and is almost always active with plenty of plans and leadership opportunities. However, they do not often listen to the plans of their spouse or follow their spouse's lead because of their defense mechanism of denial. They may deny not only their spouse's desires but also the importance of their spouse's emotional needs or their valuable opinions. They believe that their own desires are more important.

They lustfully take in all the food, money, and deals they can get and do not balance their money or their health very well, despite their spouse's concerted warnings. They often have angry outbursts, tend to stubbornly withdraw without processing a conflict, and may indulge in dabbling in other relationships or addictions without much remorse since they tend to fixate on vengeance when in stress. They may polarize their spouse for their imperfect ways of loving them and guilt them for small imperfections, overqualifying their own giving at the same time.

At this level, the Eight desperately needs a weekly therapy session with a logical and straightforward coach or counselor they respect so they can sort things out and balance their desires with the needs of their partner. They may also need a mood stabilizer, and they should seek medical care if they are struggling with anger management or abusing their family verbally, physically, or both. Seeking balance is important so they don't lose their generous attitude or the innocent, childlike love deep inside them.

An Eight in Relational Dysfunction

A dysfunctional Eight in marriage may be coping through addiction to substances or sex, and often to more than one thing. They may also have developed a health issue because they don't minimize food intake or know how to do anything with moderation. They may even have trouble with the law or in business. They've often created enemies for themselves, feeling that they are outside the law.

They may be isolating and moving away from friends at a rapid rate, as well as trying to make their spouse withdraw, so their spouse feels they cannot be married to them any longer. They may be so vengeful over issues they've had with their spouse that they divorce them or frequently threaten them with various consequences. All of this can make living with an unhealthy Eight very difficult, and when given the opportunity, some spouses will leave.

If You Love an Eight

If you love an Eight, remember, they are going to love you hard and long if they feel you can be trusted and respected. This is, however, a rather big "if" because, as most Eights know, they have often lost trust at an early age and are on their guard. Plus, they can be very severe about even small mistakes. But they can receive insight about this and make headway as you set boundaries and demand respect.

Remind your Eight of being self-controlled versus always lust-fully going after more. Encourage them to find a balance of being helpful and not demanding. Remind them to pause, breathe, and connect instead of playing God or following only their gut. Your gentle but firm reminders and boundaries can help you both to shape a powerful and mighty love.

Type Nine Levels of Relationship Health

A Nine in Relational Health

A healthy Nine in marriage is strong, fun, thoughtful of others, and typically quite social. They know how to stand up for themselves with clarity when their spouse, family, friends, or co-workers hurt them or forget them. This forgetting often happens due to the Nine's peaceful countenance or perhaps others' envy of them. However, the Nine finds ways to show up with vocal tonality and with their strong, solid body language. A healthy Nine is both peaceful and present. Because of this healthy self-assertion, the Nine does not hold in a huge amount of instinctual anger. Therefore, there is very little that goes unprocessed between spouses.

The Nine is not constantly fixated on comfort but is able to seek their own active goals without being pushed. Their energy is great, and they are full of love. Many Nines even become major change agents in the world, especially surrounding issues about which they are passionate. This is often referred to as their "right action." Right action does not mean they have a corner on truth, but because they often consider others, observe before speaking, and are attuned with the world, they have wisdom to share.

A healthy Nine is able to show initiative not only because they are awake to their own and others' needs but also because they allow time for bodywork. They enjoy creative social outlets for fitness and love completing their routines each day, which definitely involve both comfort and work. Many Nines take walks every day to achieve this presence as well as make prioritized lists regarding what needs to be done in life and marriage.

They try to lean into their spouse's love languages and have regular times for relaxing, not only alone but also with their spouse and family. They are part of a communication pattern that is positive, logical, and emotional. They take two or three hours a day to rest and retreat but stay focused and alert otherwise, not running from conflict but engaging practically in both speaking their needs and compromising with the needs of their partner.

In terms of helping their partner to shine or glow, Nines give their spouse the beautiful gift of comfort, harmony, structure, fun, and goodness even in situations where one of them may be quite tense.

A Nine in Relational Stress

A moderately distressed Nine in marriage doesn't value themselves in terms of their capacity or potential but overly values their own comfort. This leads their spouse to feel that the Nine is spoiled. They do not typically prioritize bodywork in this space and may passive-aggressively devalue the needs or requests of their spouse and their own legitimate needs. They narcotize themselves to responsibilities or anything that makes them feel even mildly disharmonious. Therefore, they can ignore important discussions and feelings, instead tuning in to comforts, work, alcohol, television shows, and sleep instead of prioritizing relational presence.

This Nine isn't always insightful about how they're behaving because they don't consider matters important enough to talk about, don't feel self-efficacy, or simply forget. Because they love comfort, they can get mad at their spouse for not caring about them or seeing their desires for comfort, feeling like if they don't have it, they will be anxious or break the harmony they desire at all times.

Sometimes they forget the good things their spouse has done and have a long memory for when their spouse hasn't listened to them or has otherwise missed the mark. They haven't yet identified that awakening from their comfortable and sluggish lifestyle will help to dissipate the typically undigested anger that sits inside of them. This awakening will also help them to inhabit self-soothing techniques to decrease anxiety.

The Nine needs time every day for self-care, especially physically. If they don't get it, they will go back into their slothful and unprioritized routines, allowing life and their marriage relationship to simply happen to them. This is in place of being a healthy Nine—an active, brilliant, multifaceted, diplomatic, emotional, and powerful force.

A Nine in Relational Dysfunction

A dysfunctional Nine in marriage is typically a peacekeeper, not a peacemaker. Even their peacekeeping is limited to a noncommittal stance without any real involvement in the care or justice of others or self. Because of the deep sadness and the feelings of being lost and forgotten that accompany a decrease of energy output in the world, the Nine often becomes victim to an addiction, has withdrawn to the point of being almost comatose, or is involved in a relationship with a partner besides their spouse. This is a result of their passive-aggressive style of dealing with conflict in their marriage and allowing prospective suitors to charm them without resistance.

A Nine in a state of dysfunction has often lost the hope that their partner will ever hear them and possibly also the hope that they are even worthy of being heard. Before a partner is aware of how badly they are feeling, they may leave. They have perhaps had a crisis of faith without attempts at thoughtful reconstruction. They have decided that peacefully self-soothing is the only way to be comfortable in the world. Thus, they retreat into hedonism instead of addressing issues. In this state, they are stoic, amoral, and passive-aggressive, yet they retain the belief that it is right for them to be comfortable and to have basic humanitarian care. No longer will they reach out for sexual intimacy, affection, or the relationship; instead, they spend time lamenting about how unseen and unheard they are.

If You Love a Nine

If you love a Nine, you have found someone who is gentle and peaceable and who truly doesn't want to hurt anyone else. The energy they spend merging with your needs and those around them, however, makes them very tired. Even if you have to rouse them or give them attention, encourage them to get body care and to get on a daily schedule. Tell them that their voice of love, wisdom, and gentle but strong diplomacy is needed in the world.

Remember to take time out to listen to them. Also remember that when they get loud, they are feeling either unheard or anxious. Address those particular issues as best as you can and lull yourself out of the calm they bring you to truly hear them. Remind them to make daily prioritized lists, offer them options if they can't decide on something, and don't rush them. Give them time to consider and stay present. Soon enough, they will have preferences and opinions and consider your needs.

Reflection on Your Type

Now that you've seen your type or types from both the brightest and the harshest lights, it's important to understand that growth takes time. No one is immune to falling into patterns of at least moderate distress at times. It's okay if you've seen yourself at the lowest points. Take a deep breath. Knowing is a great first step.

I also encourage you to be honest about where you're at now so you can shine all the brighter. Take courage! Insight may yet bring some change, and I hope you've found some great reminders and steps for yourself in these pages.

If you read about your spouse as well, you may be eager to tell them you've got a treatment plan for them. Remember to let them do their own work across many days, weeks, months, and years. Jane Austen's wise warning to us rings true: "I wish, as well as everybody else, to be perfectly happy; but, like everybody else, it must be in my own way."[3]

With your new insights, try your hand at your best way. Take the partner tips into consideration, using what is helpful and leaving the rest behind.

Finally, don't shame yourself if you're on the lower levels of health in your type. Remember that we all fall into some shadow versions of ourselves at least occasionally across times and seasons. Keep this book handy for such seasons so you have specific steps to climb back up to health when you're down. Remember that growth comes little bit by little bit. Thus, there is grace when you fail to do things well.

AFTERGLOW

Illuminate: As you've looked through your own as well as your partner's types, how have you both perpetuated some unhealthy systems in your marriage, such as moving too fast or lacking momentum?

Spark Up Heart-to-Heart Conversation: After this critical gaze, open your hearts to each other. No one is perfect. What is it that you love about both your type and your partner's type?

Glow Brightly Together: What will you each do every day to get self-care spiritually, emotionally, and physically so you can give better in the world?

3

Learning to Love One Another with Head, Heart, Body, and Soul

Their wholeness came upon them as a rush of light, around them
and within them, so that she felt they must be shining in the dark.

WENDELL BERRY[1]

When my father met someone, he sized them up with the classic eye
squint of legendary cowboy Clint Eastwood in his infamous "Go
ahead, make my day" speech. Sometimes he was right to approach
defensively or with caution, but when his overactive internal threat
system was activated, my mom did what most of us intuitively do
when our spouse leans too far in one direction. She balanced him.

For instance, when Dad read too much into someone else's behavior and made plans for swift retribution, Mom kept him from
making many grave mistakes. John Gottman, the world's foremost

marriage researcher, confirms that this is exactly how we as spouses help one another on an ongoing basis. Indeed, he took it a step further: "Neuroses don't have to ruin a marriage. If you can accommodate each other's 'crazy' side and handle it with caring, affection, and respect, your marriage can thrive."[2]

In your family, too, the protective layering that bleeds down generationally from your father and mother is both unrelenting and natural. We must not imagine that these family patterns are from just one generation back but from many, many generations in most cases. This protective overlay is intended to safeguard us from challenges we might face. Because of this, we often have strong tendencies that our spouses can help us to balance.

As you can imagine, with such a strong overlay in our home with our father, we children were wired for strategic defense just as he had been. As we grew up, news channels blared to remind us of the latest updates on world warfare. We were given Stratego and chess sets for Christmas. Family days off were spent in museums or in contemplative nature at the Metroparks, but never at the wave pool since Dad had a friend drown in high school, and his own mother, most likely a type Six, had given him an overlay of extra protectiveness for his family. We spent our humid summers in the many libraries of the local area, traveled to Canada for more parks with no swimming, and even visited a nuclear power plant for a safety tour.

Instead of what most American kids from the eighties and nineties wanted—pool time, skating, amusement parks, or Disney World—we were shown epic documentaries and war dramas like Goodfellas and JFK. Many an hour was spent at the gun range surreptitiously eating Cheetos and reading with Mom while Dad did target practice to make sure we were well protected. My mother and my best friend's mother balanced him with multiple trips to the mall and Skateland, as well as with a wonderful Sunday ritual of a bookstore run after church for the latest installment of The

Baby-Sitters Club, R. L. Stine's Fear Street series, and Christopher Pike's mystery series (all of which Dad moaned about in protest as a classic literature instructor).

As a wife and mom today, I've allowed both of my parents to influence my parenting. Although you can regularly find me watching *Parks and Rec* with my teens or laughing over the antics of Greg in *Diary of a Wimpy Kid* with my son, now I'm the one asking the kids to watch *Gettysburg* or visit the Henry Ford Museum when we go back to Michigan.

It may be a bit humbling to admit you're a lot like the parent you swore you'd never be, but if your spouse mentions it, I wouldn't argue too hard. We do rub off on each other, after all, and some of it is good. It's okay that sometimes with the good, the harder aspects rub off also, as long as you're willing to work on them.

I used to resist when Wes told me I was a lot like my dad. I've learned over time that he's often right. At times I can project too many negative shadows and memories into our married life, just like Dad did. I've also come to understand the pain my dad carried a lot better since the early days of my marriage.

The good news is, we get not only unhealthy but also healthy patterns from our predecessors. I've become okay with recognizing these patterns in myself because compassion toward self and others tends to run more fluidly after age forty.

Our hard-to-break patterns and stories are why we *must* have others in our lives to help bring out aspects of healthy living. Humbling as it is, this is where marriage can help quite a bit. Our spouses are unusually good at detecting ways we are unbalanced, right? Our strengths and weaknesses both become very well-known to them over the years.

Instead of our parents, it's our roommates, children, spouses, and partners who now stand alongside us in our best and worst moments. Quite frankly, as John Gottman indicated, it is our distinctive role as partners to gently balance one another so we don't go crazy. In terms of the ways we engage in the world, we each tend to lean into primarily a body knowing, a heart knowing, or a mental knowing, which we unpack below.

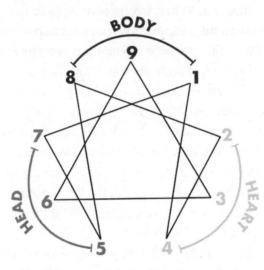

The Centers of Intelligence in Marriage

Regardless of your personality types, you and your spouse utilize your head, heart, and body senses to aid you in moving through the world, yet each of you tends toward one of them more than the others depending on your type. Important synonyms for this group of three are Enneagram "triads" or "centers of intelligence."

The term "centers of intelligence" sheds further light on the fact that each of these orientations toward engaging with the world is a unique skill and way of knowing intelligently. Similar to personality types, there is no hierarchy of intelligence centers, as there is more than one way to engage with one's surroundings.

When you use all three centers, you avoid the shadows of yourself in multiple ways. Each center's function has its strengths and weaknesses, its healthy and dysfunctional uses. Any one of them can be overutilized or a blind spot.

Now it's time for the exciting part of using the intelligence centers in marriage. When we look at the flow (and the glow!) of our relationship as we interchange intelligence, we're open to using even more of ourselves. When we are leaning in to one another to share our gifts with an awareness of our blind spots, we can use our gifts with synergy. *Synergy is "the extra energy, power, success, etc. that is achieved by two or more people, companies, or elements working together, instead of on their own."*[3]

So let's take a deep dive into the Enneagram centers of intelligence so you can learn how to best reach the heart, body, and mind of one another in your relationship.[4]

The Heart Triad Spouse

The particular gift of those in the heart triad—Twos, Threes, and Fours—is reading others intuitively. This is a skill that we all need for survival and thriving. As it turns out, most of my fellow peers in my counseling program were naturals at teaching this skill, and many of them were heart types. They showed me what it means to open one's heart to vulnerability and connection in a rich way. We cried with each other as we told stories of loss. My best friend, Stacey, another heart type, once cried for me on a phone call when I did not have the sensation to cry for myself.

Because these experiences were so foreign to me, I'll never be able to state with words how wonderful it felt to be loved like that for the first time. It felt like opening up a window to an aspect of the universe I hadn't felt in a very long time. Integrating the skills of heart attunement as they were modeled for me made my own clinical and coaching work much richer. It did the same for my marriage.

However, using *only* our hearts potentially exposes us to dangers of all kinds when our critical thinking skills and physical body or environment are under the threat of attack.

Heart center types naturally want a lot of attention in a romantic relationship. Remember, this is not intentional. It's rooted in the fact that they are often making up for low self-esteem and attempting to earn love and identity. Since heart types also react with shame and sadness or find that feelings of neglect are aroused when they're not in health, sometimes they overreact with feelings only, giving over power and even their very self to others too easily and ultimately neglecting thinking and bodywork.

If you're a Two, you try to help the world in order to find your worth through giving and overly attend to others without boundaries. As a Three, you try to aggressively and futuristically earn your worth by displaying wondrous new iterations of yourself through work and achievements. As a Four, you try to show the world you're invaluable because of your creative and different style, and you withdraw internally, focusing on the past when you're disappointed by the world's misunderstanding of your very sensitive heart.

A good tip for heart types in marriage is to try allowing wisdom and thinking into your strategies of getting healthy so you're not basing everything on feelings, which will ebb and flow. Another important action step is to add in bodywork as an essential aspect of your daily routine, so you can also regain a sense of self apart from others as you learn to enjoy the autonomy and physical strength that is often seen in body types. Celebrate the fact that the good parts of your heart help you some, but don't give them *all* the power.

Remember, if you're a person of faith, prayer can help you think clearly and create in you a clean, trusting heart toward God first, before you give it over to anyone else. Start your days by asking God who you can and should speak to or help. As Psalm 90:12 says, "Teach us to number our days, that we may gain a heart of wisdom."

If their focus is only on gaining another person's affection and attention, types in this group will never be fully able to relax since people are fickle and change on a whim. But when they instead put faith in God's wisdom and love despite their partner's changing moods, they stand on something much more sturdy. It is so wise for heart types to take some time to nurture a spiritual life and to truly see that their people are loving them in their own ways.

In sum, heart types tend to read the emotions of others well. They can thus pick up on the moods of their spouse and can manipulate to get their needs met covertly. They need to awaken their physical senses with fitness, healthful nutrition, and rest. They also need to grow mentally with productive thinking, such as list making, strategizing, and time management. They can pause and take deep breaths as they begin to activate these body and mental centers and invite themselves into the process of choosing to see their spouse love them in their own ways.

Relationship Tips and Pitfalls for the Heart Center Types

Type Two

Twos in particular can be manipulative to ensure they get the love they feel they need. As Twos are in the thinking-inhibited Enneagram stance, they are also not always able to think critically about the past or future. Instead, they remain stuck in the present, dealing with only the relationship right in front of them. This can allow them to overbook, lack boundaries, push themselves too hard, and forget the good behind them already as they cling to others for all their needs in the here and now.

Since often they intuitively feel others' pain, when a partner is grieving a personal loss with work or extended family, the Two wants to help. However, they may find their intent to help goes unappreciated, unnoticed, or unwanted, especially if their partner deems the Two likely to ask for a return on investment that feels pushy.

Why do they push for love in manipulative ways? And what creates the stuckness of this positioning in their heart work? Emotionally, Twos fear rejection and may have faced abandonment issues growing up. In addition, they frequently repress their own anger, sadness, anxiety, or hurt feelings to please the people in their culture since they are generally compliant and relational. They want to do what is deemed right and good by society.

However, their repressed feelings manifest in ways that feel manipulative, prideful, and controlling to those around them, sometimes unbeknownst to the Two. Even when they seek only to display the happy feelings, they don't always succeed. This overcompensating behavior can mask depression and create marriage struggles.

Type Three

The Three focuses attention on tasks and goals to create an image of success in the eyes of others. They identify with their work, and their aggressive-assertive stance type is ever forward moving, sometimes erroneously leading them to believe they are what they do. This kind of thinking may cause them to lose touch with who they really are.

Their thinking pattern centers on doing and accomplishing tasks. Though they feel the emotions of others, they avoid their own unconsciously because doing so helps them to get things done. When they slow down and get in touch with their feelings, the magnitude of them can be difficult to swallow. They may realize at times that they are loved for what they do and not who they are, and this may result in sadness and anxiety. Threes tend to express impatient anger if someone or something gets between them and their theoretical goal.

Threes have a desire to be loved for who they are and get harsh when the sensitivity underneath their confident exterior is breached.

Additionally, they tend to be fast-paced workaholics and find it very difficult to slow down and "just be." They can be extremely productive and effective because of their laser focus on getting things done and reaching their goals.

Their passion, or vice, is vanity, which comes across as a concern for their image and life in the eyes of others. Vanity motivates Threes to present a false image to others as they tend to shape-shift into whatever image is perceived as the right or most successful one for the given context.

Type Four

Fours focus attention on their own feelings and memories, the feelings of others, and interpersonal connection and disconnection. This is what qualifies them as being part of the withdrawing stance and locks their gaze in a past orientation to time, for better or worse. They typically feel a sense of deficiency about their own worth or seek idealized experiences or qualities they perceive as outside of themselves. Because of their feelings-type rejection issues, they can test their partner frequently to see if they are loved for who they are uniquely.

Fours love and value a wide range of emotions. However, their thought life is focused on what is missing emotionally, whether positive or negative, and is also shaped by their constantly idealizing of what isn't and what could be. They appreciate meaningful interactions of all kinds and have keen aesthetic wisdom, but they tend to dwell in feelings and, if they are especially stuck, are often cold and melancholy when approached by their closest attachment figures. They do this hot-and-cold interacting as a way of testing their partner.

Fours have a wide range of emotional sensitivity, at times reserved and withdrawn and other times energetic and exceptionally joyful. They are emotionally intimate, empathic, and intense. Fours

97

generally aren't afraid of conflict and may even enjoy it to an extent in marriage. They will work tirelessly when they are passionately connected to something. They see what is missing and speak to it.

The Head Triad Spouse

The particular gift of those in the head triad—Fives, Sixes, and Sevens—is a troubleshooting thinking style. Those in this group can process what to do in an emergency within a moment's notice and deliver ways to keep the couple and their family safe and well cared for with acuity, speed, and courage.

The head center regulates our thinking function, analyzing abilities, and logical processing. It allows us to take life in through words and mental imagery, which further allows us to process our thoughts with intention. For head types, this offers designated routes or paths for feeling safe in the world and allows them to connect with others while building a sense of safety and community together.

Often their fast thoughts are stressful in life or marriage, and the stories they tell themselves run away without them. There are several ways thinking types handle this pressure. Fives try to reduce the possibility of feeling things by pushing away from everyone and seek inner knowledge to help them through. Sixes find a way to secure themselves in the relationship to feel safe. Sevens quickly rationalize or reframe sorrowful circumstances to temporarily push all negative thoughts away.

Even as I wrote this chapter, Wes brought breakfast and opened my home office window for me to look out. When I am in an active thinking mode (which is often), he reminds me to pause, breathe, and see the world around me. After learning the Enneagram lessons we'll unpack here, he now knows this space is as natural and favored as breathing is to me. Still, he's going to lovingly hold me accountable for not staying there. He's an ever-present totem beckoning me back to the land of the living, and that's where his favorite space is. In fact, even when he's not here, I can hear his voice in my head reminding me to take breaks and intentionally pour into my people.

Even if you're not exactly like me, the world we live in is very headspace oriented, so I bet you've seen some similarities. This hyper-modern culture began in 2007 with the advent of the iPhone. In his book *The Ruthless Elimination of Hurry*, John Mark Comer reminds us that these days, most of us in the Western world get lost in this frenetic headspace in some way.[5] Post-COVID, it seems just about everyone has a way they like to retreat.

The only problem is, when we're stuck exclusively in this headspace, we often incorrectly sense that more mental planning or insight, more online connections, and more analysis mean more safety. Ironically, an imbalance here actually disengages us from the other important aspects of true survival that only an in-person heart-to-heart or body-to-body connection with each other can bring.

In her book *The Wisdom of Your Body*, therapist and researcher Hillary McBride reminds us that, along with our heads, our hearts and bodies are a fluid part of us that must not be cut off.[6] Yet in our strategizing and analyzing, this is the very thing that happens. We process data, telling internal and verbal stories both about what could happen, what might have happened, and what we need to do to make sure everything is okay.

I don't want to shame you if you learned to overanalyze in your cultural or family setting. On the positive side, these stories help us to fill in gaps. Most humans learn by storytelling. Indeed, some statistics remind us that we learn from stories twenty-two times better than just lists.

As a thinking type, I stand daily on the following verse in Philippians 4:8: "Finally, brothers and sisters, whatever is true, whatever is noble, whatever is right, whatever is pure, whatever is lovely, whatever is admirable—if anything is excellent or praiseworthy—think about such things."

Our minds need a release through emotions and also through the body. Workouts help in this latter aspect, of course, as with all types.

While strong thinking is a gift, overuse or misuse can lead to becoming overly analytical, having anxiety attacks, or spiraling down into analysis paralysis, panic, or paranoia. Rather than allowing only these adrenaline-heavy solutions, those in the thinking triad need to face their fears with a few regulating deep breaths and some healthy boundary-setting as needed. However, instead of trying to create only security (which this world cannot always give), they need to seek faith, something not easy for thinking types, who often replace God with their own constructs for what will make them feel safe.

Contrary to Twos, Threes, and Fours, who are great at examining the feelings around them, the head triad members are thinkers and often leave their own and others' hearts out altogether. They become very focused on the practical and safe matters of life. So they need to be reminded that as long as they don't give feelings *full* power, it's very healthy to allow them in for a short time, even if they don't seem very practical to express. Head types may even allow themselves five minutes a day not only to think about or worry about negative feelings but to *process* them through writing, speaking, or crying.

Relationship Tips and Pitfalls for the Head Center Types

Type Five

Fives tend to be anxious about the outside world and thus try to isolate themselves, which is why they are considered part of the withdrawing stance. They often end up obsessing over a partner in the early days, but as time goes on, they may find one of the following issues arise: losing interest altogether; feeling rejected, overloaded, or maxed out most of the time; scrutinizing actions and money habits of their partner; or spending a lot of time in fantasy retreat, idealizing their research or another ideal partner.

They must realize they have to give in order to get and understand that no relationship will ever satisfy perfectly. They often look back with doubt on the past and the memories of being overwhelmed, which is what constitutes them in a past-time orientation stance. Also, they should try to understand that no amount of research will build back the consistent lack of confidence in their abilities that they feel deep down. Instead of trying to hoard knowledge or goods as a defense against this perceived lack, a Five must learn to be content with "enough" versus "all." They must trust God for more each day, or at least try to gain faith in the process of resting and actively sharing, which will help in storing the new information they gain.

Emotionally, Fives have trouble moving from their withdrawing, past-focused, feelings-inhibited posture to a place of emotional processing, even when their spouse or others have tried to share this truth with them. This is because they fear their lack of competency, which may be the consequence of facing humiliation, illness, bullying, a gross lack, or a deep sense of overwhelm that was hard to recover from.

A Five covers themselves up as a form of protection so they will not be hurt again. This unfortunately can create the self-fulfilling prophecy of rejection that they are trying to avoid.

Type Six

Sixes tend to be anxious internally. Although present in their time orientation, they are still inhibited in their thinking as their

intelligent minds are often naturally playing out worst-case sce-
narios. Because of this, they have trouble centering their minds on
the fact that their spouse does not always want to be controlled or
have a plan for everything. They also must learn that people will
let them down, but that does not mean those people can never be
trusted.

A Six must learn that life is even more of a curious adventure
when they learn to take some things in stride. If they allow fear
to limit them so that they create perfect boundaries and curated
relationships, then there is very little growth. But their dependence
on authority figures can be tempered with increased trust in God's
ability to work through even the biggest changes of plans. More
importantly, they should seek to understand that these unexpected
changes can be wonderful beyond their comprehension.

The spouse of a Six does well to let them process fears for a little
while each day but then move them into gratitude and planning.

Type Seven

Sevens tend to deny their anxiousness and thus are always keeping their minds and bodies busy in the aggressive-assertive future
stance. They are also mindful of the fact that they often use the
defense mechanism of rationalization, maneuvering themselves
into others' good graces. However, eventually they will have to do
the work it takes to keep a relationship afloat, whether that means
contributing to a savings fund, slowing down and doing chores, or
facing the actual anxiety that lies beneath their joy and fun. This
is no simple process, considering their spouse often expects them
to carry joy into their relationship. However, as with all processes,
there must be a balance and a mixture of gifts with virtues, which,
in the case of Sevens, are joy and sobriety.

Sevens also have to consider that they have an inner critic they
can mistake for being the critical voice of others. When they spend

a long enough time delving into their own emotions, they can learn to differentiate and work through their inner critic's cruelty with not just petty resistance but active and responsible steps. These steps can prove to themselves that they will experience grace but also must learn to take responsibility.

Sevens have a gluttonous passion, and they want to solve all their problems by keeping their minds indulged and busy with work. However, rest must be paramount since they move at such a rapid pace, and they must also find a way to settle their minds through stimming. Additionally, they can find peace and rest by allowing God's plan to unfold, even if it feels boring or painful. This process may even help them realize their gluttony was actually causing a lot of the same pain they were running from. In marriage, they often need to work on self-soothing behaviors so they can listen better.

The Body Triad Spouse

The final triad is the body triad, also called the sensing triad, doing triad, gut triad, justice triad, or anger triad. These individuals are gifted with quickly and instinctively noticing things in the sensing world that are "off." Their reactions tend to be physically felt. They also have a keen ability to clarify complex details and act to bring rightness and justice to the world. If those in this triad—Ones, Eights, and Nines—are hurting in a relationship, they typically experience frustration before vulnerable feelings. They have a desire for safety even if they don't always tell others about it. Ones and Nines, however, don't even feel like admitting anger to themselves. Perhaps they haven't been given attention or they think anger is an unhealthy emotion that should be concealed. At any rate, anger *does* need expression, just not all the time.

The body center regulates and manages the five senses. Body types feel things in their body immediately and viscerally. This allows them the ability to understand their environment keenly, detect the needs of others, and determine the best strategies given their situation and surroundings. While this is a positive thing, overuse or misuse can lead to controlling behaviors, blindness to others' views (including other body types with differing views), and loathing of imperfections in self or others.

I saw the desire for justice in Wes from our earliest days of dating. He often found one lonely student in our huge lunchroom full of cliques and would beckon me out of my comfort zone to sit with him as he tried to make the person feel seen. This aspect of him is also an absolutely essential quality for his work in the medical field. Often his reading of a person's body language saves their life as he brings an almost imperceptible diagnosis more clearly into focus.

Body types also make mistakes, of course. They can make a quick moral judgment that is quite black-and-white, forgetting to look for the outside variables in a situation or failing to recognize that everyone has a different vantage point. They can let aging or cognitive function work against them in their stubborn insistence on seeing the world only through their lens, instead of allowing compassion and a growing maturity create in them a desire for empathy and more neuroplasticity. They may miss a richer form of problem-solving that involves contemplation in the mind and heart. Without balance, some of them may burn out in their zeal to promote right action, even as they mean well.

On a positive note, they also *need* to check in with their bodies, especially since they are coming to learn that nonverbal communication makes up, by some accounts, over 90 percent of human connections.

As you may have gauged from early chapters in this book, body types tend to read the five senses in the world many times faster than head types, who tend instead to be quicker with scanning for safety. In addition to reading the body language of others with accuracy, Ones, Eights, and Nines also have a clear sense of justice and rightness.

Ones repress anger, a "bad" emotion. They don't let anyone see it until the anger is so thick or they're so angry it comes out as passive or active rage. Eights prepare to meet a challenge with their anger directly. No one will find them vulnerable to it, even though sometimes they do need to temper it. Nines get tired or sleepy, narcotizing pain through TV or food.

If you're in the body triad, remember that instead of letting your gut instinct provide you with all the information about what's right and wrong, allow your thoughts to logically slow you down and create a truer picture than just a simple black-and-white photo. Add color by considering other people's gifts, which differ from yours, and perhaps remembering when they cared for you, if imperfectly.

Accessing your heart is also huge if you're a body type. It's important to show feelings to a few safe people regularly. You are so strong and guarded against hurts, but you need healthy releases. Beyond that, the people in your life need to see your heart, not just your anger, which shows even if you think it doesn't. Since you store and react to stress in the body, working out, massage, or whatever other meditative or helpful bodywork you enjoy is critical for your release and success. In Jesus's culture, people could walk and work their feelings out more naturally, whereas now, our only exercise may be our fingers on our phones as we work from home, order takeout, and drive in automatic cars.

Body types need to let God play judge and fight for social justice when they need to settle down and rest. That doesn't mean they stop serving well or using their mighty gifts, but it does mean they don't play God by deciding the fate of others or holding out resentment when justice doesn't fall the way they feel it should.

Body types tend to process from their instincts. They pick up on a strong sensation of right and wrong quickly and recoil when something feels wrong to their senses. They need to work on sensory integration and tolerance of the ideals of their spouse. They also need emotional awareness, regulation, and self-soothing. Adding in bodily stress release via fitness helps, as does relaxing with their spouse with levity and fun. They can pause and take deep breaths as they begin to activate relaxation and release full control of their environment.

Each of these body types has the capacity to exert great strengths, suggest order, and care about truth and justice. However, they all struggle with a misuse of the instinctual anger that frequently rises up when they don't balance and take time to do bodywork on a daily basis. Fortunately, there are great techniques and skills to utilize when encountering some of these issues.

Relationship Tips and Pitfalls for the Body Center Types

Type One

Ones focus on noticing errors in themselves and their partners in the present time. They are in the thinking-inhibited compliant-dependent stance. This is especially true as it pertains to their own internally generated ideals and their overt concern with discerning right and wrong. Their reliance on rules, structure, ethics, and morals can be rigid.

When frustrated, Ones often tighten in, protecting their autonomy and becoming rigid and negative in their bodies. This tension can last a long time since they tend to repress anger, which stems from the belief that they are "bad" when they experience anger. When they do finally get the courage to express it to a spouse, the spouse has often already felt the anger in some way and is sensitive to the One's critique. This can further a couple's polarization.

At this point, Ones may express hostility since they believe their actions are correct, and they will try to force things into conformity. For this reason, it is important for Ones to practice the inner work of releasing control and their desire for perfection to God and to get their bodywork in. Furthermore, they should engage in healthy arrow work.

Type Eight

Eights focus attention on power and control and who has each. They often surpass all other types in terms of both energy and the desire to control. They are in the aggressive-assertive stance. They focus on the big picture and have a disdain for details, leaving those to others. They see the world in terms of strong and weak, and they believe this dichotomy pertains to both emotions and physicality. They access anger but misidentify it with softer emotions, especially if they're not doing their inner work. They do not like to be told what to do and typically engage in black-and-white thinking as a means of satisfying their desire to protect themselves within their internal dialogue. That said, when they are directly challenged, Eights often do very well at managing emotions, and many have reported that a calm overcomes them in an actual crisis.

They will also protect the people they care about with their strength, energy, and power. However, sometimes they forget to acknowledge their limits and avoid involvement in anything that will slow them down, even when it costs them their health. Some Eights even take stimulants to avoid decreased strength, though this is only in states of dysfunction.

Their passion is lust, a passion of expression and intensity in all manners of stimulation. It is a drive to fill up their inner emptiness

107

through physical gratification. This can be sexual or any other type of gratification the Eight focuses on in excess.

Type Nine

Nines focus attention on others and what is going on in the environment. They desire to avoid conflict and achieve harmony. They are past focused and in the withdrawing stance.

Nines typically tune in to what other people want and do not have a clear sense of their own agendas. They don't like to allow conflict in and will work hard not to come out of their "turtle shells" or to rock the boat in any way. They don't like breaking harmony and want to go with the flow. They tend to forget that conflict is part of the necessary flow of life. In contrast to this withdrawn posture, at their best, Nines can be thought of as a great river, which can carry everything along with power and hidden strength that has been stored and reenergized with their incomparable body type current. It is surely a dichotomy that Nines have a reservoir of energy but access very little of it. For this reason, they are generally the most tired of all the types.

The passion of Nines is sloth or inaction of the psyche. This is more about inattention to the self and inertia of the will than it is about their spouse forcing them into this position. Therefore, they need to bravely and wisely engage. The alternative—inaction and avoidance of conflict—may cost them their own identity and selfhood. Furthermore, it opens the door to depression, addiction, dissociation, and full inaction.

It's time to reflect on what you've learned thus far about finding your glow together. Make sure you carry grace for one another and yourself, as doing your work takes a lifetime. This, however, is why marriage is long. Keep taking small, intentional, and brave steps to learn, to grow, and to be curious about one another's and your own types.

AFTERGLOW

Illuminate: Now that you know your centers of intelligence, what are your blind spots in terms of those?

Spark Up Heart-to-Heart Conversation: How may your missing some of the gifts of all three intelligence centers be unintentionally hurting each other?

Glow Brightly Together: Can you hold one another accountable and hold yourself to your blind spot work even while you know it is very hard to change deeply ingrained patterns?

4

Fighting for Your Survival

Balancing Your Differing Instincts

If it weren't for second chances, we'd all be alone.

GREGORY ALAN ISAKOV[1]

Grandma Chris, my namesake, was fun and quirky, only wore black, and according to family lore, never ate and never slept. She was vain, told stories of all the men who had lived and died for her, and swore by coffee, sweets, and very little else. She would wander through her neat-as-a-pin home that was filled with chairs and davenports covered in knickknacks from the old country of Croatia. She often muttered, "I don't sleep" in a piteous little voice, bemoaning occasional blackouts in between games of rummy, stories, and lots of coffee and exercise. She was a character, to say the least.

When my mother struggled with mental health issues, as an infant I was sent away to Grandma's by my father so he could work, tend to Mom, and care for the older siblings, who were more self-sufficient. Grandma and my step-grandfather, Al, lived in the automotive town of Flint, Michigan, where I spent many fond times.

Grandma's history was a huge part of her. Her parents were non-English-speaking immigrants during the Great Depression, and she told us many stories of their plight. Her beloved mother, Domenica (Minnie), and her aunt Teta (Frances) left all they knew behind on their tiny island, Mali Lošinj, off the warm Istrian peninsula of Croatia. Though today Mali Lošinj is known as "the island of vitality," when the women came from it, they were as exhausted and unglamorous as most immigrants then and now. In essence, they were tired of eating potatoes and grateful to be beckoned by Lady Liberty herself. In their long lifetimes, they went from being considered Austrian to Italian to Yugoslavian to Croatian nationalists, and in the time of immigration, they were considered the lowest on the totem pole of Croatian families in frigid northern Michigan.

These boardinghouse tales, as they came to be known, scared us kids half to death as we heard about Grandma's harrowing escapes from death and all its friends. She had grit, and her legacy was one of rags to riches. Her vivid retellings both gave us chills and thrilled us to pieces as we shuddered and guffawed with her.

One such story was of a man who had been betrothed to my great-grandmother Minnie. Apparently, he wanted revenge because she hadn't married him. My great-grandfather slept with a gun under his pillow in case this man ever showed up from the old country. Eventually he did, when my great-grandfather was out in the woods. This man asked my grandmother, a young child then, to get a drink from the bootleg cellar. While she was gone, he stabbed Minnie. Grandma ran for a doctor and then watched as the doctor successfully stitched her mother up right on the kitchen table. True to their island's motto of vitality, they all lived to tell about it. Minnie and her sister Frances lived to ninety-nine and one hundred, and Grandma to ninety-five.

The other story that stands out most to me is a foundational one for our family. Grandma and her siblings were starving during the 1920s and stole carrots out of their neighbor's garden. When the neighbor caught them, she yelled at them. Grandma survived on just a bit of flour, sugar, and coffee, while some of her many siblings did not live to tell their own tales. Perhaps this was why Grandma did not eat much or sleep much in later years, working incessantly instead.

Despite her traumatic life, Grandma learned to rise up and work hard. She saved money to buy her own home and cars with her General Motors pension, as well as to put my father through private Catholic schools and all the way through Boston College's graduate school. Because of her and many other World War II "Rosie the Riveter"[2] women who fought with grit for respect and survival, women today have more access to equality than ever (though there is still work to be done).

You, dear reader, surely know the anguish that came from your own ancestors and older relatives who sacrificed so much for you to be at least somewhat leisurely reading these pages. Older generations have fought hard for you and me to be here in many mysterious ways that we will never know, as secrets also die with each generation. But whether the stories are stated or left untold, the generations that came before us have made their marks on us, and their influence is both undeniable and enormous. Whether our families were part of one of the historic diasporas, escaped slavery, survived wars, or faced other traumas, our family narratives shape the ways we feel safe in the world. As we listen to what we're told about the past, we find ways of bringing honor to our ancestors' arduous journeys.

The same is true for our spouses. Not surprisingly, my husband, Wes, had very different family stories. These heritage tales helped him to trust the group process so much more than I do. Because there was no work in the hollers of eastern Kentucky in the 1950s,

113

his great-grandparents and grandparents carried their faith with them as they headed north to look for automotive work in the Detroit area. His grandparents' nine children grew strong on the farm and labored under their parents' instruction. Unfortunately, they too had tragedies with which to contend. A car fell on Wes's grandfather when its jack broke in the 1960s, and as he was the main breadwinner, the family's cupboards were soon bare.

It was the church and the surrounding community who came and filled those cupboards to the brim in the following weeks and months. In fact, we still have the picture of Wes's mamaw and some of her kids standing proudly, fathoming at God's provision from their generous community of faith—dazzling hope within tragedy.

This outpouring of love greatly reinforced the need for faith and group participation in my husband's family. To this day, my husband is never happier than when giving to, serving with, and sharing with neighbors and church friends and families. This social instinct is a wonderful calling, as it echoes the golden rule: "Do to others what you would have them do to you" (Matt. 7:12).

Wes's presence in my life has reminded me and our children of just how important it is to find a good spiritual and community home. From our earliest days of dating, he helped me to find love in social communities too, sometimes in those I had written off (including my church family, who had scorned my own family during my mom's season of mental health issues). It was and is healing to be part of a community of people who love God and who help one another.

How Your Family-of-Origin Instincts Influence You

These stories are historical pieces of our family legacy that have been passed down to us as totems from which to learn. As we look at the three instincts couples may have developed through their own natures or inherited from their families, we must realize each deeply ingrained style of surviving has its place. Nature and nurture are both at play here, though there is often a strong family link, as Bea Chestnut and Uranio Paes speak frequently about. Even if the instincts are not directly inherited, they may be passed down in the way that families emphasize, teach, and model their particular instinct—as "the" way to live life.

As you and your spouse look at your own preferences as well as your previous and current culture to dig out what is important, true, and relevant (nature *and* nurture), you must decipher the messaging and take forward only that which is prudent. The rest you must depart from. This isn't always easy, especially with our biology tugging at us.

The hope is that as we all do this important work, the next generations will take the lessons from their elders and move forward with them carefully. As Lin-Manuel Miranda and Opetaia Tavita Foa'i's beautiful lyrics in *Moana* remind us, we will "tell the stories of our elders in a never-ending chain,"[3] as well as learn to use that knowledge to chart our destined paths. Like Moana says, "I am everything I've learned and more."[4]

It's imperative that you add new information to these tales. Your ancestors with their cautionary tales did not expect you to follow their instincts exactly. As you understand and sort through their stories, you can honor your ancestors by hearing their lessons—both the exemplary and the cautionary tales.

As you and your spouse consider the stories and legends from your own familial history, remember that as we merge in marriage, we most often prefer our own ways of behaving in the world to dominate that of our nuclear families. And why not? Our families have used these systems to survive, and we are here as living proof.

Yet these instinctual responses often have a deeper hold on us than we realize and may require greater exploration. The deeper ridges of survival that these stories contain—how to survive when threatened, what defense mechanisms we favor when there's a family argument or crisis, and so on—inspire us to be better humans and to carry the family mantle with pride and honor.

What Are the Instincts?

There are three ways of survival within the context of the Enneagram, and these "instincts" refer to our biological drives:[5]

1. Self-Preservation (SP)—taking care of one's personal or immediate family resources
2. Social (SO)—relating to others generally and in social groups
3. Sexual or One-to-One (SX)—one-to-one bonding and other types of fusion experiences

It's important to note that each of the nine Enneagram types can embody any of the three instincts most prominently. They do not vary by Enneagram type. Typically, one instinct is dominant while the others remain repressed or, at the very least, more difficult to access. When using this layer of the Enneagram, finding balance concerning the three instincts in your marriage is the goal.

There is good news and bad news when it comes to these instincts. Just like with your typology and the ensuing glow of your combined hues, you reflect your best and brightest together when you learn from one another's very powerful instinctual sequence and learn to balance your own.

Although balancing is tough because change is hard, many Enneagram researchers believe that in most cases we instinctively *choose* a spouse from a different instinct to learn from their way of seeing the world, thereby increasing our potential to carry out a healthier and more balanced lifestyle and to pass those genes on to future generations. Since we become more like each other over time and through seasons of marriage, we not only influence one another but can have a blind spot together. It's fascinating to find a collective shadow that neither of us is aware of as another vital area of growth in marriage.

When Bea Chestnut was a guest on *The Enneagram and Marriage* podcast in 2022, she suggested that we are able to find important aspects of ourselves when we face both our personality shadows and the shadows of our repressed instinct.[6] She also discusses shadow elements of personality in her book *The Complete Enneagram: 27 Paths to Greater Knowledge.*[7]

As you consider which of the three instincts you and your spouse each typically exhibit the most, I also want you to pay attention to areas of shadow that you may both be balanced in. For instance, if you've helped your partner to become more self-preserving (SP) over time and they've influenced you toward sociability (SO), note whether you have a shadow of the pair bond between you (also called the sexual, the intimate, or the one-to-one instinct, all of which are abbreviated as SX). This is what Wes and I face, so we plan a date night every week and discuss how often we want to be intimate to bring that balance. Otherwise, we could be two parallel lines sharing only our well-defended self-preservation instinct and the social instinct, yet missing the one-to-one connection with each other we need so desperately for human connection and attunement. In marriage, this one-to-one safe attachment is the very reason we work so hard to protect ourselves socially and otherwise.

Each of these instinctual strengths and shadows are much bigger than merely the direction of our marriage relationship. We can also miss the one-to-one bonding time with our children or friends because of the particular ways we shine and shade ourselves.

Self-Preservation Instinct (SP)

If you're self-preserving, you tend to pay close attention to basic needs of food and/or shelter for yourself and your people because you realize how important basic survival is. The bottom line is, you like to make sure you feel good in your body. You do this by saving resources, both materially and energetically. You usually put on your "oxygen mask" and put your self-care needs first, and you're skilled at anticipating those needs for the future.

When this instinct is repressed or only some areas are emphasized, some of its corresponding needs are forgotten altogether, such as showering, saving money, having basic clothes or furniture, or eating well. Whether SP needs are over- or underemphasized, the goal is to rebalance, as we all need healthy amounts of self-care, planning, and rest.

In marriage, a person with a high SP may want and need to spend more time recharging on their own or with their spouse at home. Of course, balance and integration with other instincts are lifetime goals and practices to pursue, but this person's safety needs must also be honored.

Social Instinct (SO)

If you're social, you tend to pay close attention to the social groups in your life and how you fit into them. You realize how important to survival that give-and-take in society is, whether it be religious, political, environmental, hobby related, career related, or otherwise. You stay away from unsafe groups, and you like to align yourself with both familiar groups as well as groups that resonate with your standards and values, sometimes to the demise of your individual time or one-to-one relationships.

When this instinct is repressed or only some areas are emphasized, some of its corresponding needs are forgotten or neglected, such as paying attention to what's happening socially, voting, and being social, and we may ignore our wider family or community group responsibilities and world concerns. Whether SO needs are over- or underemphasized, the goal is to rebalance, as we need to pay attention to how we can come together to help the world as a community.

In marriage, a person with a high SO will likely do more out and about in the community, both on their own and with their spouse. They will feel refueled by this time and want to regularly have plenty of social engagement with people who have similar values and life practices. They love to sharpen one another socially, and their need and appreciation of others' good influence upon them cannot be underestimated.

Sexual or One-to-One Instinct (SX)

If you're sexual, you tend to place your greatest attention on your one-to-one relationships in friendship and in marriage and family. You desire connection and realize how important this nurture is to your personal and family survival. You also like to make sure you're attractive and powerful in your relationships so you are not taken advantage of with any form of abuse. Sometimes you may do this to the demise of your time to yourself or your involvement in community care.

When this instinct is repressed or only some areas are emphasized, some of its corresponding needs are abandoned, such as the desire to have close bonds, to marry, to enjoy intimacy—sexual or otherwise—and to work through conflict. Whether SX needs are over- or underemphasized, the goal is to rebalance, as we need to pay attention to the quality of our relationships. Avoidant behaviors breed further anxiety and depression in humans, who were made for close, nurturing bonds.

In marriage, a person with a high SX may long to spend more time in one-on-one dates and in connection with their partner and others they are close to. They both want and need time recharging with their spouse, directly facing them, touching, or completely engaged. They will desire both sexual and nonsexual time with their spouse, depending on their nuanced life experiences and desires. In many cases, small, close groups are also welcome. Of course, balance and integration are lifetime goals and practices to pursue in marriage, but a person with a high SX may prefer to spend more time recharging on their own or with their spouse at home.

Instinctual Sequencing

You probably appreciate and even experience all three of the instincts from time to time—that's great. However, one of them is usually dominant for you and more than likely even overused. Another one, your secondary instinct, is probably slightly less dominant but still often used, and the third instinct is the one that typically falls last in your personalized instinctual sequence. It may be rarely used or even repressed. The goal is to balance all three of the instincts quite closely, so your secondary and third instincts get as much experience and attention as the first. When you do this, you greatly increase marital stability and widen the opportunity for family survival skills, and your influence in the world is shaped in a much healthier manner.

So, as you read, the question stirring in your mind may be: Can we really balance instincts that have become so deeply ingrained across a generation and genetics? Yes, in small increments and across seasons. Your spouse may be able to help you with this since, as I mentioned earlier, we often pick a spouse who is gifted in other areas.

Let's bring this experience to life with an actual couple's story.

Instincts in Marriage: Clara and Marcus

Marcus was SX dominant. He loved his one-to-one time with his wife more than anything in the world and grew jealous of her time with friends or her extended family. His family had a history of anger issues, and he grew up feeling like he had to be loud and persistent in the world to get anything he needed.

Some people found Marcus exhausting due to his loud voice, what they called a pushy attitude, his flashy attire, his strong cologne, and the dominance he brought into most conversations. This was particularly true for his wife, Clara, who was SP dominant and felt overwhelmed by his control, anger, and many passions.

Although Marcus instinctively chose Clara for her soft, sweet ways and Clara instinctively chose Marcus for how special he made her feel, the disparity sometimes embarrassed and overwhelmed them both. There were deep marital concerns on both sides. Could they trust someone who didn't seem to understand such an important piece of them?

After a time of intentionally balancing their instincts, Clara noticed that she was more willing to go to social events with Marcus, especially if he was willing to talk with her one-on-one just a bit or there was a quiet corner she could retreat to if she felt overwhelmed.

Marcus loved this agreement, since he loved that she was out with him more. He felt a thrill at the prospect of showing others that they were a model couple, and he truly had a heart to inspire friends and family to pour passion into their marriages. Clara's willingness to lean in here also gave Marcus the courage to give her free time to rest or to see her friends without him complaining. In fact, across the years and with intention, he even began to settle down and relax more on his own at home and to find friends to hang out with.

One final positive result is that Marcus felt like he didn't need to dress or act as an SX quite as dominantly since he was secure with the mate he had. He didn't feel Clara pushing him away, and they were both able to relax instead of living married life in such a heightened defense system.

Refining Goals with Instincts

Though our primary instinct is primary for a reason (it has helped us to survive!), when we begin to feel safe in marriage, we can rely on it slightly less and even learn from our spouse. As we can see from Clara and Marcus, when we lean into balance, it helps to regulate our partner too. A basic proponent of family systems therapy is seen here: When one part of a system shifts, the other also has to make a move.

Remember, in your marriage or relationship, the ultimate goal is to find your instinctual balance with your partner so that together your sequences are smooth and well-balanced. With two people in the mix versus just one doing their individual work, it takes a little longer, so expect small shifts over time. Make some room for error and expect to fall back into old, familiar patterns too. Be gentle and encouraging and take lots of deep breaths and pauses when you need to let your partner grow at their own rate.

Despite the long process, a growing marriage is a safe place to discover and try out other variations of finding safety in the world. It expands our ability to grow and to help others uniquely. In other words, it helps our glow.

We may also find safety and trauma healing together due to the collaborative work we do over a long period of time to find a healthy balance. This has the greatest likelihood of occurrence when we intentionally grow and take breaks for dates and adventures. Part of our stretching here will also allow for the acceptance of our differences in life as we find that we are sequenced differently in terms of our instinctual preferences.

In time, you and your partner will see your beautiful balance. If you're getting healthy, it will inspire them to get healthier. Whether and when they choose to do the work is up to them. Remember, there are seasons. Set your boundaries accordingly so you don't expect your spouse to be everything to you, but offer the tools to them for growth as well.

Another important tip I want to share is this: Don't tease a spouse who is sequenced differently than you. If you don't think one of the instincts is important—to the point that you're making fun of your spouse—it usually indicates you have work to do in this area. Again, I can't emphasize this enough. Do your homework rather than trying to push your spouse into theirs, and get good therapy or coaching from someone who understands these systems.

When Instincts Go Gridlock

Surely these instinctual differences in marriage and relationships account for some of what John and Julie Gottman call "gridlock," a concept that describes couples who have diverging opinions on what would be best in any given situation. Although some ways of processing conflict will lead us to full agreement, a whopping 69 percent of marriage issues fall into this area of difference.[8]

It's also imperative that we help one another to find the balance of the instincts. When we lean too heavily on just one or two of them, we often have personal and relationship blind spots. However, when we're working with each other, we need to learn soothing tips. For instance, when you feel flooded with a gridlocked issue that's tapping into one of your instinctual defenses, your system senses a threat. It will typically respond in a familiar format to combat the threat, since we've been fighting for our survival since the very beginning of our lives. You've heard of the fight, flight, freeze, or fawn responses, right? Well, this is exactly what we do here when we feel like our survival mechanisms are in question, even in marriages without trauma.

How do our instinctual responses show up when we feel challenged? Everyone is different to a degree, but in most cases, our bodies tighten or our nervous systems are shaken, our breathing becomes less regular, our heart rate goes up, and we need frequent breaks to try to manage our stress responses. Gottman researchers have also concluded that if your heart rate exceeds one hundred beats per minute in conflict, you won't be able to hear what your spouse is trying to tell you no matter how hard you try. Therefore, soothing yourself and one another is essential for getting out of your gridlock.[9]

How will you try to soothe one another? "Try" is indeed a key word as seasons shift, life experiences differ, hormonal patterns change, and different things work in different moments. It's vital that you and your partner talk about what feels good to you in terms of soothing behaviors.

It can also be helpful to attune to one another's bodily responses and make decisions slowly if one or both of you have triggers with trauma or even just complex family stories that lead you into more cautious decision-making. As you're learning to balance, touch can be a helpful way to relax. Offer an extra-long hug, massage one another, touch foreheads, lightly rub one another's temples, hold for an extra-long kiss, scratch one another's backs, or do some simple breathing together. You can regulate one another's trauma patterns in this way by watching your spouse's breathing and doing the same pattern, or you can stretch or take some deep breaths together for a few seconds.

Consider taking thirty minutes independently for a cooldown. John Gottman has done multiple studies on this, giving a poignant reminder for how long it can take you to settle down once your system feels flooded. If you have trauma, there are excellent full-scale treatises on how to soothe yourself and each other through difficult or traumatic situations. Aundi Kolber's *Try Softer* book and workbook are some of my favorites for connecting with the heart and body safely.[10] I also love the research in the aforementioned *The Wisdom of Your Body* by Hillary McBride. Both authors are trained therapists who have worked with a multitude of individuals with varying trauma.

AFTERGLOW

Illuminate: Do you have any early memories of how your instinctual sequence got its start in your life?

Spark Up Heart-to-Heart Conversation: Which one of the instincts seems to be more repressed for you? Journal or talk about how you overuse your dominant instinct and underuse the repressed one in your relationship and life.

Glow Brightly Together: What is one hope you have for yourself and the next generation or the world socially (SO)? Take small, tangible steps in becoming a bit bolder in all three of your instincts so this is more likely to occur.

5

Throwing Shade

Addressing Relationship Conflict with the Harmonic Groups

There is no perfect soul mate, no flawless lover.
We are all stumbling around, treading on each
other's toes as we are learning to love.

SUE JOHNSON, EDD[1]

The Office almost started a big fight in my marriage.

From the time we checked in to the hospital, preparing to have our third child, Jack, the map was charted. As a thinking type, I was ready and determined to have my baby just the way I had planned it: watching this hilarious show.

If my first and second labor and deliveries were hard (and they were), I hoped the delivery of my third baby would be a charm. *The Office* would be a good distraction for me when the pain was great. It was positivity for the win, and Wes and I were off to the races.

As a medical professional, Wes knew that even with all the optimism in the world, our bodies don't always do exactly what we tell them. Plus, in our first two delivery experiences, we had done the natural birthing classes as well as lots of reading, and I had still required Pitocin and an epidural in both cases.

With this backstory in mind, the first thing Wes did to make sure all went well with my labor and delivery was to find me a doctor who had a good reputation and bedside manner. The next thing he did was to brush up on how to help deliver a baby. He had no interest in obstetrics, but he had delivered one baby in medical school. When I heard him listening to YouTube podcasts surrounding the process, I got a bit nervous and laughed it off, playfully calling out, "It's all good! I've got this."

By the time we set off for the hospital on the morning of March 29, 2012, I was armed with my laptop and ready to watch my show. We watched Jim and Pam's love story and Dwight and Angela's antics for several hours, and I laughed most of my way through labor. When it was time for the epidural, I switched to yet another form of stimulation for a bit and blasted Coldplay's "Yellow" in my ears as the needle went in.

When it was closer to the time to have the baby, Wes gently but logically encouraged me to stop watching *The Office*. He knew I was getting close to delivery with his five senses acuity. As anyone in an extremely painful position knows, my patience was growing thin. I wanted to scream, but since neither of us felt safe with strong emotions, I gave him a glare, shut the computer, and gritted my teeth.

But there was a problem. Our quiet logic and positivity did not give away signs of the emotional distress we were in as we saw labor approaching. We gently told the nurses it was time and we could tell our son was coming, but they didn't believe us. No one in labor could be so nice and polite. The doctor was nowhere to be found, and they said not to rush him.

Wes and I waited for them to page the doctor. "You have time," they said. "Hold on."

So I did what I do when I feel like I can't trust anyone else in a survival situation: I went within to find inner joy. However, there was no joy to be found, only emergent need. I was hooked up to an epidural, couldn't feel my legs, and was in a state of dependency, ready for my hospital birth for better or worse.

"It's time, Wes," I said. I looked him square in the eyes and asked with rare emotional vulnerability, "Can you do this delivery without the doctor?"

"I think so," he said. "Can you give me a minute? I need to get the room ready."

I let out a breath and paused. "I'll try."

He asked the nurses to let him scrub in with gloves and a gown, and he made sure the room was sterilized as much as possible. Within a matter of minutes, I was pushing as he reached in and moved the head and shoulders into position.

Our son was born right then, and we named him Jack Lewis after Wes's favorite author, C. S. Lewis, just as our daughters had been named after some of my favorite authors. Wes placed Jack on my chest to begin nursing.

The birth was a success—a precious, fun, and beautiful moment we shared. There was both lightness and logic at work.

Indeed, positivity and logic are two of the three important elements of good problem-solving skills in conflicts. However, a third element, passion—the willingness to put emotional stakes in—is also needed.

Because of this missing ingredient, Wes and I didn't lean in with our voices, which ultimately may be why we didn't get the help we needed. Thankfully, there were no emergencies or complications. Otherwise, the outcome of this story would potentially *not* have been so joyful. Looking back, we realize this with sobriety.

I'm going to put my cards out on the table here. Emotional problem-solving is a blind spot for our marriage because it's a blind spot for our pairing. We love our comfortable gait of working hard with logic and positivity, but while those qualities are great, we hit walls sometimes when we forget the third angle.

When we remember that there are three main styles of processing conflict and that our spouse often has a different path than we do, we honor their experience as well as our own. If we don't, in our own efforts to heal pain with our often broken, shadowy style, we widen the chasm to problem-solving even more.

Instead of finding a communion of our gifts, we fall into the shadows of seeing only one way of doing things, and that's just not going to work long-term. What's more, when we do this, we once again fall into the fundamental attribution error of believing that *our* particular style of dealing with life's upsets and conflicts is the one good way.[2] Resentment builds, and we begin to form narratives of individual victimhood, not realizing that we *each* have things to teach one another about how to solve the problems in our lives as they occur.

At this point, our bond suffers as we break into factions, our work suffers as we forge ahead with fewer moving spokes in alignment, and our family suffers under the tension of our stubborn and limited views. Worse, we pass on to our kids and friends the belief that our partner's way of coping with the world is insufferable compared to ours, and our loved ones miss out on having a more robust problem-solving style of their own. Truly, our light shines the brightest together when we integrate diverging, healthy conflict styles.

When we don't each lean in here, we find ourselves in a conundrum not only about the problem at hand but even over *how* we argue. We're no longer glowing vibrantly together but in a shadowland of sorts, burning out and sometimes even losing our footing among the dark pathway.

It's important that we take a deeper dive into the three different ways of approaching conflicts as well as the corresponding types that typically choose each style. In the world of the Enneagram, we call these Harmonic Groups.

What Are the Harmonic Groups?

The Harmonic Groups of the Enneagram illustrate general methods that specific clusters of types utilize to address and process conflict, both individually and within their relationships. All people behave differently in conflict, but the commonality is that we care deeply. This is important to remember, especially if there is a clash between partners who are situated in different Harmonic Groups.

So how do we deal with conflict?

Well, some people are vibrant, loud, and reactive because they want their partner to give them attention and don't think there is another way. This may include a variety of emotions, yelling, and/or tears.

Others want to approach everything carefully and with logic so nothing important gets missed and emotions don't cloud their path. There may be withdrawing emotionally, harsh objectivity, or a stoic, silent approach to solving issues.

Lastly, some people try to remain positive, feeling that being negative will hurt their relationships in some way. There may be people-pleasing, rationalizing, or going within.

There is wisdom in all the styles, but it's maximized when the three methods of dealing with conflict are blended so that none of them overwhelms a couple.

According to traditional marriage research, withdrawing is one of the absolute worst things a couple can do in marriage when it comes to conflict since it draws them apart. But here, too, there is a caveat. Not every marital issue needs to involve an emotional root canal. Sometimes withdrawing is healthy for a bit. Partners may need space and time when they are struggling. Healthy withdrawal involves setting some parameters, which include terms of endearment so their partner does not feel abandoned. For example: "I will go away for thirty minutes, but I will be back, and I love you," or "We may be going to bed for the night, but I love you so much. When could we talk about this some more this week?"

In *The Wisdom of Your Body*, Hillary McBride emphasizes how couples need to decrease withdrawing in order to inhabit their emotions and to find support from one another. When they lean too far on others for a perfect solution, they miss the opportunity to grow themselves.[3]

As we study this topic a bit more systematically and apply it, we must also approach it without sabotaging each other's growth unconsciously. For instance, if I'm used to my partner responding to conflict positively and I've grown comfortable with it, I may try to block them from the important work of incorporating logic or healthy emotion.

As you process this information with care, review the illustration and lists below, which summarize the three inclinations toward conflict and show how these often manifest in the nine Enneagram types.

HARMONIC TRIADS

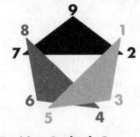

♥ **Positive Outlook Group**
♥ **Competency Group**
♥ **Reactive Group**

The Harmonic Groups of the Enneagram

Group	Types	Tendency
Positive Outlook	Two, Seven, Nine	They try to reframe everything as "no big deal" or otherwise as positively as possible.
Competency	One, Three, Five	They desire competency and use logic in an argument.

132

Group	Types	Tendency
Reactive	Four, Six, Eight	They view everything with reactivity in hopes their spouse will do the same.

With this overview in mind, let's take a deeper look at the tendencies, benefits, and challenges of each group's attitude toward conflict. Please keep in mind that one of these styles may be needed more than the others at any given point. In a crisis, for instance, logic may be needed first. But balance is the goal.

The Positive Outlook Group

The Positive Outlook Group consists of Enneagram types Two, Seven, and Nine. Each type maintains a positive outlook when faced with disappointment or conflict. Within this triad, each type has their own method for maintaining positivity and is unique in what they emphasize, avoid, and overemphasize. They each have a unique way of reacting to their own needs and the needs of others, but all of their reactions are framed through a positive lens.

Variations among the Positive Outlook Group	
Type Two	<ul><li>Twos emphasize their positive self-image.</li><li>They avoid their own needs and disappointment.</li><li>They overemphasize the needs of others and neglect their own.</li></ul>
Type Seven	<ul><li>Sevens emphasize positive experiences and their environment.</li><li>They avoid their pain and their role in creating suffering so as not to lose their positivity and ideals.</li><li>They overemphasize their own needs and are easily burdened by the needs of others.</li></ul>
Type Nine	<ul><li>Nines emphasize the positive qualities of others and their environment. They value the importance of others over themselves.</li><li>They avoid problems with their loved ones, their environment, and their own lack of self-development.</li><li>They overemphasize the desire to meet the needs of others while they are asleep to their own needs. This imbalance causes them to become internally passive-aggressive.</li></ul>

Advice for the Positive Outlook Group

Be aware that you tend to overlook and sometimes even deny important problems. Realize that sometimes conflict is needed and it's beneficial to face a problem without putting a positive spin on it. Boldly work through the pain.

Drawing on the strengths of the Competency and Reactive groups can help you generate the best outcome when problem-solving and addressing conflict.

The Competency/Logical Group

The Competency Group (often called the Logical Group) consists of types One, Three, and Five. Each of these types has competency in mind when faced with disappointment or conflict, but they all put emphasis on different ways of being competent and manage their feelings in a unique manner. Each has a different orientation toward systems and rules but relates in a competency-minded way.

Variations among the Competency Group	
Type One	• Ones emphasize competency by being correct and sensible.
	• They avoid feelings by repressing and denying them instead of channeling them into activity.
	• They want to follow systems and rules and can get upset with those who do not adhere to the same rules.
Type Three	• Threes emphasize competency by being efficient and outstanding.
	• They avoid feelings by repressing them and focusing on tasks. They also look to others for feeling cues.
	• They overemphasize work within a hierarchical system but also want to work on their own, outside of the system. They often have little patience for rules.

Variations among the Competency Group	
Type Five	• Fives emphasize competency by becoming an expert and having knowledge.
	• They avoid feelings by detaching and staying in their head center.
	• They reject many traditional systems and often overemphasize quite complex logical systems they create. Like Threes, they have little patience for rules.

Advice for the Competency Group

Be aware that you tend to deny emotions. Realize that sometimes addressing feelings directly is necessary, and it's important to fully process disappointment. This can also help you have a better connection with others.

Drawing on the strengths of the Positive Outlook and Reactive Groups can help you generate the best outcome when problem-solving and addressing conflict.

The Reactive Group

The Reactive Group, also called the Emotional Realness Group and the Intensity Group, consists of types Four, Six, and Eight. These types believe passion is the most powerful method of showing care. Each of them has strong reactions and also needs reactions from others when faced with disappointment or conflict.

Variations among the Reactive Group	
Type Four	• Fours emphasize reactivity by vacillating between withdrawing and emotionally seeking a rescuer—someone to understand them.
	• They avoid logic and positivity because of perceived abandonment and lack of support.
	• They overemphasize contemplation and keeping others interested through limiting access (i.e., playing hard to get).

135

Variations among the Reactive Group	
Type Six	• Sixes emphasize reactivity by analyzing and assessing people and situations. They seek both safety and support (i.e., someone to rely on), but they also want to be strong and fortified.
	• Sixes fear and push to avoid being abandoned or without support, and they avoid becoming too dependent by questioning authority.
	• They overemphasize planning, commitment, and reliability to the exclusion of independence, missing any peaceful acquiescence. They stay engaged but are also defensive.
Type Eight	• Eights emphasize reactivity by openly expressing anger and seeking independence and self-reliance.
	• They avoid being controlled and dominated. They also avoid being vulnerable.
	• They overemphasize this positioning by keeping their guard up and toughening themselves against potential pain.

Advice for the Reactive Group

Be aware that you tend to overemphasize your emotions. Realize that how much you display your emotions and frustrations can deeply impact others.

Drawing on the strengths of the Positive Outlook and Competency Groups can help you generate the best outcome when problem-solving and addressing conflict.

Now that you've seen the differences in styles, let's take a peek into a couple more relationships to see how they can play out.

In one of Macie and Manuel's first appointments with me, as soon as I heard that Macie had experienced infidelity in their marriage, I handed her an absolute slew of John Gottman forms to complete. She'd had an emotional affair with another man, and Manuel had also been unfaithful. So I wanted to get some research about it.

Instead of finding an eager research participant, however, I was met by a mother who was very tired and in the throes of life with six kids, including one nursing during our sessions. Macie needed a heart connection from someone since her husband was

136

not providing it, and she was newly trying to cut off from her affair partner. Typically positive, she had reached her breaking point, and she knew she had things to face. She was more interested in an emotional exchange with me about attachment and motherhood, and as you may have already guessed, she was not interested in all my forms. She actually laughed in my face when I handed them to her, and we connected over this funny faux pas.

Manuel was a professional athlete who traveled a lot and lived a life of hustle, bustle, and charm. He was an ambitious achiever and also in the throes of a midlife crisis. He didn't want his wife to leave him, especially after his series of one-night stands came to light along with his wife's affair. Although he didn't have the emotional lens for communicating, he expressed his feelings for his wife through creativity in gift giving. As an Enneagram Three, he produced. These gifts and productions were brilliant, but Macie, a passionate woman, was left wanting.

The marriage work we did together was hard, scary, and ultimately beautiful. It was all about bringing in a new skill set to take the place of maladaptive coping styles. In this case, we brought in a skill set that wasn't intuitive for them (or for me, for that matter) but was nonetheless integral: emotional processing.

When this kind of balancing work happens with intention, the rewards are far-reaching. All parties experience tenacity, hopefulness, and emotional attunement. I am in awe of this kind of healing and of those individuals and couples who are brave enough to pursue the passion, intimacy, and commitment needed to form a healthy bond. It makes me feel very thankful to be in the sacred realm of relationship work.

So much changed for Manuel and Macie as we completed their work. Macie was able to depart from the almost previously hopeless messaging of "He doesn't understand my heart, so I'll seek love elsewhere." She also realized her affair partner didn't want a life with six kids any more than she wanted to leave her family, but she did want to see that her husband truly cared with his heart. Now she realized he did, though they each cared differently. Manuel opened his heart vulnerably, crying in our sessions and sharing that he had pursued sexual encounters as a result of feeling desperate for nurture. Macie softened when she saw his pain, even though she insisted he get further treatment and accountability. They both ultimately learned that they needed to lean into their emotions as well as a logical, loving, positive narrative about their family and who they could become together. Only when they had all three components of conflict solving were they able to write a new narrative for their marriage.

A few years later, another couple, Allison and Gabriel, had a different communication struggle. While they had both emotions and logic in their marriage, they had very little positivity, and I could see why. They'd had a terrible tragedy in their lives: the loss of their elementary-aged son.

As a result of that tragedy, Allison began to do life in a trancelike state. All of her motions, previously saturated by logic and a fairly stoic attitude about life, became even more rote and systematized. Her attitudes were really only a cloak of living, and she began to withdraw to cope. There was logic, but all expressions of the sad heart were pulled inward. She feared losing herself entirely if she had another loss or even fully faced her current one.

Gabriel was almost as far to the other end of the emotional spectrum as he could be. He shed tears in our sessions. He wondered aloud if they had been cursed, and he shouted with agony about how the doctors didn't do justice to the life-saving measures they'd attempted. His expressions, while authentic to him, overwhelmed his wife to a great degree. Their coping patterns also exposed their blind spots, which exaggerated the gap in their two styles of communication.

Before we could move forward with logic, emotion, and positivity on any level, we had to allow for a safe space to process grief. We could not avoid it or just dance around it romantically. The couple needed to process it together and in a way they both could handle.

In times like this, when emotions need to be tended to but not expressed to the point of overwhelm, we often need third-party help to light new paths for connection as a couple that bring us toward one another in positive ways, not just to share in grief. As Gabriel and Allison were offered a safe space to share memories as well as to shed tears, we saw glimpses of light resurface increasingly. And though the loss was a part of their story daily, there were now many moments of laughter, connection, and hope for a heavenly reunion with their son as well. Allison joined a dance class for peaceful release of the bodily tension she carried, and that also opened her up for a lighter countenance. Gabriel began a daily gratitude practice and, with his great passion, volunteered time with a foundation for grieving families. Soon Allison joined him in some of the work for this ministry, and they also found new passions together, learning ballroom dance and growing in faith through their small group at church.

In couples who have the passion of two reactivity types, there is still another mystery to solve. It is a great strength to them that their bond or their glow is intoxicatingly bright. Yet they can also create a lightning effect with tempers flying if they do not intentionally balance in logic and positivity. This is especially true where there is a family history or cultural overlay that leans toward solving problems with violence.

As we know, families and marriages are complex. Suffice it to say that sometimes there are comorbidities outside of just a style of communication to discover and discuss, such as trauma, affairs, neurodiversity, cultural issues, and mental health issues. Remember to take it one step at a time as you and your spouse work together for healing.

As you can see in all the examples I shared above, there was a discrepancy in problem-solving styles. You likely remember when you, like me, missed the mark in your balance of these styles. If you don't choose to learn from this and to balance all three styles, when a relationship rupture occurs, the conflict gap can be likened to the aftermath of an earthquake. Though the initial wound or trauma may be over, there is still a gap between the faults. Whether it's a tiny fault line or a gaping wound, most couples will create and experience some sort of trauma together.

Some couples have one partner who is actually doing their work and is less reactive, cold, or overly optimistic. They're coming back to a place of warmth, compromise, and care. Yet the other partner is stuck in the rigidity of a failure to thrive for one reason or another, often to the frustration of both partners. I empathize with both positions, but I ultimately hope that you get some good counseling support if you're feeling frozen in place or even going backwards a bit.

A few years ago, my friend Carla, a creative type Four, somehow turned a photograph of a simple wheelbarrow into a special and creative analogy displaying the process of change. I hung the photo in my office to use with my clients, as it clearly illustrated how easy it is to get stuck. The wheelbarrow was situated on a bumpy dirt path, journeying through a prairie down the well-worn course even though the grass around it would have been a smoother ride. The ruts were deep, and it would take continual, intentional lifting and balance to maintain change over the course of the journey.

It's much easier to take the old, bumpy path we know—the one with divots, the one that is familiar, the one that keeps us sunk into well-worn deeper, darker spaces. Remember this as you start to get liftoff. God can still use you in the dark, and he is still with you there. But he loves to move you into healthy spaces as you do your part to remain intentional and lifted up on the journey. Give it time and take lots of deep breaths and pauses instead of simply surrendering to what is easiest or most familiar as you and your spouse move into healthy new adaptive patterns together.

AFTERGLOW

Illuminate: Which Harmonic Group is your conflict style, and which do you suspect is your partner's? Discuss this together if you're both willing.

Spark Up Heart-to-Heart Conversation: What is important for each of you to learn from the other Harmonic Group while holding back judgment?

Glow Brightly Together: What is your commitment to making the changes to balance all these conflict styles, even if it's a baby step you have to return to many times over?

6

Soul Care and Marriage

The Vices and Virtues

Laws and principles are not for the times when
there is no temptation: they are for such moments
as this, when body and soul rise in mutiny.

CHARLOTTE BRONTË[1]

Even inside the good work we can do as couples to balance instincts, conflict styles, and intelligence centers, despite our best efforts, we often hit another type of wall: our Enneagram type's vices (or passions) and fixations. When we feel internally threatened, not only do we come at issues with the aforementioned aspects of ourselves, but we also deal with our type's particular emotional ways (vices/passions) and mental ways (fixations) of crying, "Mutiny!"

143

Whether we fight, take flight, freeze, or fawn due to these automatic thoughts and feelings, our particular unhealthy Enneagram emotional vices and mental fixations slip into action unremittingly, especially if we're not intentionally aware of them or trying to balance here.

Let me differentiate the vices and fixations. Our vices are emotional and a response to the sorrows and losses in our lives that bring a hollowing and sad effect. When this despair hits us, or the "dark night of the relationship soul" haunts us during a particularly bleak season of life, these very personalized vices make empty and unconscious promises to deliver even when we have good relationship tools.

Our thinking patterns likewise tempt us to take bypasses and shortcuts to allowing sadness to be worked through. Instead of feeling the depths of pain and then rising up, we often use mental distractions—fixations—to help us through the tough points.

Like Charlotte Brontë said, body and soul can and often do revolt most when we are in seasons of trial. However, instead of delivering on all they have promised for us, our vices and fixations only leave us more stuck than ever. They are temporary Band-Aids covering the process of actually delving in and doing the work of allowing our body's alert system of feelings to help us solve our problems. But virtues and holy and healthy ideas will return us to a hallowed state as we enter the immersion work in the stages of our Enneagram Glow.

Virtues and healthy ideas come by you taking personal agency for feeling your feelings, then knowing what to do and doing it. While I can't assist you in actually walking out the steps to your virtue, I can help you with general tips and specific directives for your Enneagram type in your vices and fixations. Both of these processes will guide you to pick up on individual cues that will alert you to your need.

Awakening the Inner Observer

It's time to take a look at your emotional and mental processes so you can find a layer of individual health and freedom. When you're able to awaken the inner observer and encourager over the inner critic, you're learning to see yourself as God and healthy others see you—broken but also beloved. You will pause and take deep breaths as you recognize yourself spinning out of rational and healthy control.

The work will be ongoing. Countless times you will inevitably see yourself fall into the patterns that have seemed to protect you through the ages. In harder moments of life, such as transitions or times of fear or sadness, you will notice your particular issues creeping in more. It's natural to have these feelings. Instead of just covering them with some sort of defense mechanism, spend time in simply feeling the hurt as it arises and allow it to pass through your system as you lament whatever it is you need to.

When we lament emotionally, we allow our defenses to lift and the underbelly of whatever is bothering us to be seen with vulnerability. Through tears or allowing deep thought in about something, we reflect on the pain. We can thank our less healthy defenses for trying to help us even as we let them go.

We also do well to invite God into this process as we release some of the sadness and anxiety we've been carrying along the route to healing. This clearing out of sorts and lifting our problems heavenward allows us to work on creating caring, logical, and healthy thoughts about our lives. It leads us to move forward, like David the psalmist did after great loss, and metaphorically (or literally) wash our faces and eat a meal (see 2 Sam. 12:20).

Though your coming-back-to-life actions may differ from season to season, it's important to follow this cycle of lament, gratitude, and healthy life planning so that ultimately you will rise up from the pangs of anguish and find hope again.

Because the temptation to go into your emotional vices and mental fixations may always be there, it is healthy to lean on God in these moments. Though the Enneagram is a robust system and psychological model to help you see life patterns and core issues, it is not alive the way your spirit is. Thus, it can't be God to you or for you. It can't answer your spiritual demands fully.

As you embrace the wisdom and grace that follow these outpourings of your thoughts and feelings, this spiritual path of releasing your shadowy thoughts and feelings to God is your own work to do. These quiet moments with God will help you to finally heal and properly understand and narrate many of your life's deepest issues, both inside and outside of your relationships.

On the other hand, if you simply address your issues with the following vices and fixations, life will inevitably knock you down . . . hard.

Long before I learned about the Enneagram, my vice of gluttony or overdoing was already getting in the way of my life, as was my fixation of planning. That is probably true of some of your vices or mental fixations as well. Many people will find that by their early thirties, their particular styles of being or moving in the world are not serving them. Such was the case for me.

As a young therapist at the time, I thought, *I wonder what would happen if I just kept planning and pushing myself?* It was admittedly my own little human science experiment, and I thought it was going quite well. I had powerful phrases as my inner mantras.

When you're tired, keep going.
You're undefeatable.
Be all that you can be.

I didn't recognize that by pushing ahead of my spirit into exhausting mental, physical, and emotional experiences all the time, I was burning myself and my marriage out. When I was tired, my vice of overdoing kicked in, and I whispered these motivating adages to myself as needed, thinking I was quite the picture of resilience.

These phrases mixed with the cakey, full-of-preservatives, boxed protein shots I was drinking on the regular. I smugly thought I had found the secret to life since I had a formula for going nonstop that seemed to work. It wasn't that life was easy by any means, but it felt sort of doable. I paced hard, but I had lots of laughs and good times too. Either way, I did not recognize my overdoing, my lack of healthy emotional release, or my body's rhythms in the slightest.

To compensate for the mounting stress, I tried to find a road race every weekend, and I pushed my daughters in their double jogging stroller while I ran. Women can do it all, girls! Never mind the almost mind-numbing migraines that accompanied the afterparty or the heart palpitations that forewarned what was to come. My body's reactions disappointed me. Didn't my body realize I had goals to work on—like yesterday? Ugh!

At around age twenty-eight, as you can imagine, the experiment of several years of running my body into the ground blew up on me. The result? I had a somatic disruption during a nonstressful family and play therapy session with a precious mom and her daughters.

I didn't want to inconvenience them or let on that I was feeling shaky and had a throbbing, dizzy feeling. So my positivity kicked in first. I excused myself for a moment to catch my breath, finished the session, and without much fanfare, soberly finished the night out, wondering what was happening. Surely it could not be a panic attack. I was a therapist, and in my young mind, that made me immune.

Later that night, I greeted Wes and made sure my young daughters were okay. Although the throbbing and dizziness had subsided, I still felt something was off internally, so I called an ambulance for myself.

147

At the hospital, I gave myself over to a peaceful retreat reading my mom's favorite book, Laura Ingalls Wilder's *The Long Winter*. I mentally tucked away as far as I could in self-preserving mode as the doctors searched my body. Among vague diagnoses that would need no pills or treatment, I was sent home.

The same thing happened again. And again. Over time and after several more hospital runs with no clear answers, a general malaise settled over me, along with an impending sense of doom that didn't retreat altogether for over a year.

It took an integrative medicine psychiatrist on my own team at work to finally tell me what my strange somatic sensations were (and what you've probably already ascertained): stress-induced reactions to my life's pace. She put me on a vitamin C cleanse of megadoses for about a week and told me to rest and eat less sugar and processed foods. She also recommended I take a few steps back clinically since I was overdoing at work. I'm so glad for her insight because it helped so much.

As you process through your vices and fixations here, understand that insight alone does not create change. Change takes small, intentional steps, and the advice from my doctor friend finally took after a lot of other work didn't seem to help.

Also, remember we are all a bit different. Even those of us who are the same types often have different iterations of them across different seasons of our lives. For some of you, it's downright unthinkable for you to push your body so hard. One thing is sure: My vice is *not* exactly the same as your vice.

Though the phrasing for each type may be different, the overall messaging of our vices is the same. They taunt that life will knock us down if we face our sadness, anger, and anxiety in healthy ways. They tell us that we need to keep doing what we've done in the past to get by, maladaptive as it is. The problem is, living in our self-protective vices leads us to forget God, our spouse's contributions, and our collective community's ways of helping us through the storms of life. It leads us to test and retest only one way of processing the world—a very limiting and self-focused way.

Just because these vices are self-focused, however, doesn't mean they're always born of intentional malice. As I mentioned, they are often derived from early life origins, when we really did need to take care of ourselves using this now strange auxiliary route with all its detours and cutoffs.

In my own story, I had to carry myself when my mother and father were too busy taking care of themselves. However, I now have a support team and people who sincerely want to help me. At this point, thinking I am all on my own is counterproductive. Learning about the Enneagram and my vices has caused me to see this and to slowly but surely let people into my life, into my feelings, and even into my brokenness and pain on occasion, though the work is a slow and "easy does it" sort of process.

You, dear reader, also have at least some mental agency, volition, and a support system that, though it has its major stresses, has some very positive foundations as well. And we are adults now. We're no longer little kids managing our family's way of limping along. When we choose to clear the difficult emotions with lament and begin to allow healthy thoughts and strategies into our lives, and when we invite God and safe others into our pain, we receive grace, love, and practical and spiritual help.

A Surprising Sabotage

Here's what I find completely fascinating about marriage as we heal individually: Our spouses often unintentionally sabotage our growth as we begin to move out of our vices. Why? They are used to our vices and fixations and our patterns for getting out of trouble. They have grown very used to the crutches we have used. You've surely learned that humans feel safe with familiarity, and this is true both for you and your partner.

Change, even if it's positive, can feel threatening for our spouses. Some wonder if their partner will leave if they get healthier than them. Others wonder whether their spouse may be not picking up their end of the slack if they're now getting self-care or setting boundaries. Still others feel overwhelmed by their spouse sharing emotions or thoughts they've never heard before. In all these cases, our spouses need time and grace as they too learn new steps for how to respond. They may even dig deeper into vices of their own at this point. This is one of the many ways, in fact, that we bring a mutual shadow into the world instead of our glow.

It was not at all easy for Wes to hear that I was falling apart and needed to slow down just when he had gotten into medical school. Though I tried to gracefully make my exit strategy from some of my commitments, he was concerned. He had married a woman who had promised to do all her many tasks with excellence, and so far, she had lived up to that commitment. As a social-leaning One, he felt not only the weight of his own burdens but also the weight of the world on his shoulders to an even greater degree when I stepped back. Then his own vice of resentment went toe-to-toe with my newfound sobriety and slower movements.

It was a major adjustment period for both of us as we learned a new and slower, steady dance. We're still learning new rhythms intentionally across seasons as we balance our schedules together with intention, trying not to overdo but likewise trying to use our combined and individual gifts well. You too will have to learn this dance of how to let one another grow in a slow and steady manner so your individual and couple flames don't burn out too quickly.

Celebrate Your Spouse's Tiny Successes

Whatever our Enneagram type, we all grow with encouragement and positivity for the little things as well as the big. Just like a child learning to ride a bike gets celebrated for even a millisecond of balance on the learning journey, so we must intentionally celebrate the tiny, nuanced steps our spouse takes toward health, even if doing so feels weird or counterintuitive at first. For instance, perhaps your spouse was late, but instead of making an excuse for it or lying about traffic, they called to tell you. Or perhaps you wanted to talk about an issue and your spouse withdrew into silence, but before they did, they gave you a warm hug and said "I love you."

If you hang on for dear life and support the good steps you're each taking, in time you will likely see your spouse rising up from their worst vices and getting healthy. Tiny steps bless you both in the long run.

If your spouse isn't going to work on their vices, don't act better than them just because it's a good time for you to work on yours. All of us have some moments and seasons that are easier than others. When I have a particularly bad day, my husband jokes with me about finding the nearest pound cake, just like one of the characters did in *Stuart Saves His Family*. However, he also rightly expects me to set boundaries, find rest, and do my work.

Make sure you set boundaries so you can get your needs met in healthy ways every day with self-care. Remember that you need physical, emotional, and spiritual self-care, and remember that the two of you need date nights so you don't just do personal work and leave out the fun and encouragement your marriage needs. If your spouse is super stuck over time, invite them to see a counselor or coach with you or talk to your pastoral staff for more specific advice.

In addition to inviting in lament and healthy thought processes to address your vices, as you consider your mental and emotional tendencies, don't shame yourself. As the late Dr. David Daniels infers:

- Recognition that is met with curiosity and then compassion by the inner observer moves us toward integration. The term "inner observer" refers to our ability to recognize what is happening in the mind. It is the first step to being able to redirect thoughts, avoid impulsive reactions, and live a more intentional life mindfully.

- Shame and self-attack do not move us toward integration.
- Mindfully choosing to "catch yourself" in the act of "getting stuck" also helps. This is why a breathwork exercise is also recommended as a tool to become more in tune with and mindful of your inner processes.[2]

Suggested Practices for Addressing Vices

Now it's time to look at your type. The following lists will help you to create space in your life for not only addressing the vices but finding the higher virtues.

Type	Vice	Suggested Practices
One	Anger	• Pause instead of reacting instinctually when the emotion arises.
		• Create a ritual outlet for artistic expression, ideally an art form that can be perfected over time.
		• When the rage is strong, take several minutes in a private setting to scream, which is especially helpful for this body type.
		• Write out angry thoughts in the morning.
		• Incorporate a routine of breathwork.
		• Stop approximately four times a day to breathe deeply for one minute. This helps release tension and unwanted, rigid, angry emotions.
		• *These practices help a One give way to their virtue of serenity.*
		• Spousal Action: Giving your One time to digest a difficult conversation is more helpful than rationalizing. Encouraging them to get self-care or to do bodywork because you and others admire them when they do works better than telling them to do those things for themselves in most cases.

Type	Vice	Suggested Practices
Two	Pride	• Take time daily to consider your own emotions. Focus on these instead of overhelping or oversharing.
		• Reduce pride, but foster positive emotions by serving in secret. This will help hinder the mental desire to demonstrate superiority over others.
		• Avoid judging others who do not serve or love in the same way as you by remembering that energy levels, schedules, and families differ. Journal this practice if you need to spend time thinking it out.
		• Instead of manipulating plans with others, attempt to let the plans unfold as they will.
		• *These practices help a Two give way to their virtue of humility.*
		• Spousal Action: Give your Two plenty of attention and reassurance as well as terms of endearment to know they are loved, seen, and celebrated by you. When they manipulate, it's not just because of pride. They also fear that you will move away unless you see them as the best giver. They need your assurance that they are loved even when you take space.
Three	Deceit	• Take time in the morning to consider your emotions with God.
		• Verbally process feelings individually to avoid the temptation to be deceptive with yourself and/or your spouse.
		• Open up to softer and more vulnerable feelings, reminding yourself that it is truly a strength and not a weakness to bravely let your feelings inform you. Process your emotions through journaling at least once weekly as a goal (since you love goals!). Be sure to reward yourself.
		• Do not primarily focus your prayer life around the accomplishment of goals. (It's okay to have a few goals, but try to go deeper as well.) Instead, focus on how you are enough without any performance.
		• *These practices help a Three give way to their virtue of veracity, or truth.*
		• Spousal Action: Assist with growth by assuring your Three that their heart is safe with you. You can do so by telling them that they are loved for more than what they do.

Type	Vice	Suggested Practices
Four	Envy	• Address the deep emotions as they arise with a few minutes of lamentation. This usually occurs sometime in the late morning and should take between five and ten minutes at most.
		• After processing your emotions, move into a time of gratitude and planning.
		• Move intentionally and enjoy slow and interesting conversations.
		• Engage in long walks and talks with your spouse.
		• Celebrate liturgy at church and focus on the basic rituals of faith, such as lighting candles. This will help you mitigate feelings of overwhelm. Worship music, poetry, dance, and creating art can help too.
		• *These practices help a Four give way to their virtue of equanimity, or a balanced emotional palate.*
		• Spousal Action: Giving your Four time to sit in their emotions is important. Don't rush them out of those emotions just because you've moved past. They will also respond well to you sharing some of your pain after some time has passed versus you expecting them to jump into fun as soon as they emerge from their lament. Emotional recovery takes time with a Four.
Five	Greed	• Experience emotional release by setting aside time to process hard-to-reach emotions. First practice this privately, then with a coach and/or spouse in deep conversation.
		• Take time alone to process something that is challenging, such as an emotion.
		• After reflecting, share with your spouse the softer realization behind the layers of anger.
		• Attempt to share the vulnerability and love behind your calculated movements.
		• *These practices help a Five give way to their virtue of flow, or healthy give-and-take.*
		• Spousal Action: Giving your Five up to thirty minutes a day by themselves can go a long way in helping them process in their own way. You can also affirm their competency rather than tearing them down with criticism when their energy depletes.

Type	Vice	Suggested Practices
Six	Fear	• Verbally process thoughts individually. This may feel uncomfortable, but it's a good practice so you begin to trust yourself and practice thinking clearly and logically instead of allowing your thoughts to be consumed by fear.
		• Write letters to your spouse. This is an excellent practice that draws the two of you closer and helps to slow down your flooded feelings of anxiety and sadness.
		• Consider medication management if needed.
		• Try fitness and intentionally grounding yourself in the body and heart instead of flying into anxiety. These may be enough to curb your fear.
		• *These practices help a Six give way to their virtue of courage.*
		• Spousal Action: Giving your Six affirmation that they are safe with you is key. Let them know you are also concerned with security and have taken some measures to ensure the safety of both of you. This will help them relax instead of feeling like they have to parent you as you live recklessly without margin in some areas they deem important. Be demonstrative of these precautions instead of just verbalizing them.
Seven	Gluttony	• Practice pausing before speaking or acting wildly when anxious or angry.
		• Enjoy touch, soothing music, and lighting candles as a means for calming emotions.
		• Stop long enough to savor the five senses and breathe through it.
		• Spend emotional time with God daily. This is especially effective upon waking since emotions can be hard to access. Early morning is most conducive to pensive thoughts.
		• Consider medication management if needed.
		• *These practices help a Seven give way to their virtue of sobriety.*
		• Spousal Action: Give compliments when your Seven expects criticisms, offering their constant thread of inner anxiety a supportive or soothing comment instead of biting contempt. This countermove will leave them with increased relational security, giving them an opportunity to slow down more rather than spin out of control.

Type	Vice	Suggested Practices
Eight	Lust	• Pause instead of reacting instinctually. • Integrate daily opportunities for fitness release. • Incorporate weekly opportunities for playfulness and intimacy. This may include date nights and sexual intimacy. • When experiencing excess energy or anger, take several minutes in a private setting to scream. • Consider medication management if needed. • *These practices help an Eight give way to their virtue of innocence.* • Spousal Action: Giving your Eight time to lean into their vulnerability is important. When they express an emotional need, which is very hard for an Eight, don't put your own needs over what they have shared. Save this for another moment.
Nine	Sloth	• Pause instead of reacting instinctually with defensiveness, even in your own body. • Show up to meetings with a strong posture—with a presence that takes up space—leaning on your wings a bit. • Remember that other people may be reacting to your peaceful countenance and are not just being callous. • Address your mounting anger by doing regular cardio bodywork. • Try some of the following practices, which can help bring a soothing effect and allow you to become more emotionally present: studying the Bible, making daily lists, doing skin-care routines, reading interesting books, going to group fitness classes, having monthly marriage maintenance meetings, and journaling. • Consider medication management if needed. • *These practices help a Nine give way to their virtue of action.* • Spousal Action: Create space for your Nine to utilize some of the soothing activities above. Give them one day a week or month where they can choose whatever they want to do. Encourage activity, but also allow a short period of rest daily. When they share an opinion, slow down and listen with care.

Suggested Practices
for Addressing Fixations

The next list contains each type's negative thinking structures, also called fixations. The following mantras will help you to change your thinking patterns into a more productive thinking style. Reflect on your mantra and speak it out or write it down as many times a day as necessary to disrupt the negative thought cycle.

Type	Fixation	Mantra
One	Resentment	God's plan is perfect even when I have an off day, when I make a mistake, and when others aren't perfect.
Two	Flattery	When I am humble, I trust that others cannot always give in the same ways I do. I believe that I receive enough from others. I am worth learning to ask directly for my needs to be met, and I can meet them if no one else will. I can set fair boundaries and get self-care. We are all equally beloved.
Three	Vanity	I am worth more than my paycheck or my worldly successes. I am beloved by God whether I win or lose. I am a glorious child of God.
Four	Melancholy	I am not stuck in my emotions. I have the power to remember the blessings in my life at any given moment and to emerge in the world in gratitude.
Five	Stinginess	I will find competency in emotional processing when I set aside planned time to process. When I reemerge in the world, there will be synergy.
Six	Cowardice	When I step actively into courage, I lose sight of fear and am strong and wise. I can get in tune with my body by making observations through my five senses, and I can think through my problems independently.
Seven	Planning	When I rest and release my life to God's plan instead of my own, I find focus and healing, not more of a struggle.

Type	Fixation	Mantra
Eight	Vengeance	When I let go of control and judgment and trust God, I find God takes care of everything.
Nine	Indolence (Daydreaming)	When I speak up, my family and friends get to know and love the real me more, not less. I feel better when I digest my anger and get moving.

Now that you have tips for your types as you address your emotional vices and mental fixations, we can visit healing the deepest of relationship wounds so your glow can be all the brighter together.

AFTERGLOW

Illuminate: As you consider the fixations or thinking patterns of each of your types, what are you most reminded of as you venture forward?

Spark Up Heart-to-Heart Conversation: Have either of you noticed ways you've unintentionally sabotaged the other's journey away from their vice because you feared change?

Glow Brightly Together: Who is in your support community as you do this brave work of trying new styles to work out stressful issues?

7

Glow 2.0

Shining Brighter as You Heal Emotional Wounds Together

A light from the shadows shall spring.

J. R. R. TOLKIEN[1]

Kyle, an Enneagram Three, meant every word in his handwritten wedding vows. He tearfully recited them in front of all his closest family and friends. He would take care of his wife, Ashley, an Enneagram Six, until the day they died.

Ashley took care of Kyle as well, and in their first few years of their life together they accounted well for their promises. They shared love, comfort, loyalty, and the healthy rhythms of newlywed life together.

As shadows entered the story of their marriage, their early sheen of love wore away. In particular, they had a series of pregnancy losses, then two children. Ashley had also been diagnosed with a thyroid issue. Within ten years of marriage, Kyle's and Ashley's schedules had grown increasingly intense. Ashley, a head type, dealt with anxiety, and Kyle, a heart type, felt neglected emotionally. Their lives were lived in two parallel lines for the most part, as they were experiencing shadows in terms of vices and across various Enneagram triads.

Kyle had a natural proclivity for taking care of his wife and kids in material ways. He felt that if he didn't achieve, he was nothing to his family. When the stress of the marriage got worse, he only grew more distant and worked harder. This focus on success and materials increased his work hours, leaving him feeling even more neglected.

Ashley's worst type Six fears of being alone without security came true as well. She loved the comforts that Kyle's achievements brought, but she hated not feeling his comforting presence or emotional support. When she voiced her pain, Kyle was harsh. Didn't she see the ways he took care of her, sacrificing his very soul for her at times? She had *every* comfort.

Ashley began to panic, feeling like she was drowning in her own emotions and anxiety. She had everything, but the biggest thing she wanted was time with her husband, her safe place. Or was he? With every goal he checked off, he seemed to drive a wedge further between them. Ashley grew suspicious of his motives for working. What was he hiding? She began to spy on him and distrust him. He felt her animosity rising and began to deceive her about small things and big things to avoid further anger.

Though he was well-intentioned and could feel Ashley's pain with his soft heart, Kyle's interpretation of her anger at him was inaccurate. He felt that she must blame him for the pregnancy losses. The grief of knowing he could not achieve his way out of this was almost too much to bear, especially with Ashley's growing distance. On top of the guilt he felt, Ashley seemed to him to be just a shell of the brilliant person she once was. She had been quite sexual and vibrant at the beginning of their married life together, but now she had a myriad of health concerns and very little interest in or energy for intimacy in any form. When they did talk, she was almost always mad or suspicious.

Kyle asked for a separation and began considering another relationship. Ashley was livid. As someone who had taken pride in keeping her traditional marriage vows, she was shocked that he would even consider leaving, especially after they had vowed eternity together.

Ashley surprised herself by fighting hard for her marriage at this point. She woke up to more of her relationship vibrancy and convinced Kyle to get counseling with her. They made some great headway too. They learned about their problem-solving styles, they learned about one another's vices, and they even began to add more date nights, self-care, and adventure into their lives.

However, even as they improved, the setbacks were great. Ashley experienced residual worry and panic about Kyle. She remembered him taking steps to leave her at her darkest hours, and these memories kept resurfacing. She worried he would threaten to leave if she didn't toe the line, as she was misinterpreting his heart with negative storytelling. Kyle didn't know how to build the trust back either. He worried she would go within herself again and abandon him. They now required a focus on the deeper wounds in the past, not just a focus on the present or steps forward. They wisely worked with their marriage helper on the essential marriage practice of healing attachment wounds, and both were able to bravely discuss their hurts so they could start telling a more healthy story of their life and recovered intimacy together.

Healing an Attachment Wound

Immersing to Glow Brighter

Attachment wounds are long-term, negative relationship memories that haven't yet healed. If one or both of you are still carrying old wounds or scars from the past, this practice of immersing will be essential. Otherwise, the light or glow you create together will be dimmed by doubt, hurt, and wounds. In other words, your collective energy will be dragging you down, and you'll need a recharge so your light can shine as brightly as possible together.

In the case of an attachment wound, since one of the marital partners believes the other violated their belief that they will provide comfort and caring in times of distress, immersing in the work to heal the wound helps it to heal more properly. It's okay not to take on the full burden of hurt for your partner. Just do your best to walk through the stages with wisdom. As you know from earlier chapters, often our experiences are colored by our roots in family-of-origin trauma, such as when a family member treated us with shame, abuse, or neglect. It is also part of the offended partner's responsibility to break their own damaging patterns.

Frequent Causes of Attachment Wounds

Here are a few examples of issues that may cause relationship attachment wounds in your life if you don't address them together. Take a good look to see if you're operating from within a wounded dynamic unintentionally, especially if you aren't naturally in touch with your feelings.

Common attachment wounds are:

- loss of a family member or a pregnancy
- abuse

162

- a sexual affair or a breach of trust
- secrecy about pornography
- divorce in best friends or parents that makes someone feel less safe
- loss of a job or another financial crisis
- addiction
- major breach of trust with in-laws
- negligence of the relationship
- mental health issues or major physical health issues
- hurt of one another surrounding the partner's core Enneagram fear or wound

If you or your partner resonate with one or more of the items on this list or have another attachment wound not listed, it is helpful to nuance per Enneagram type as you consider healing steps. When you know one another's core type wounds, it's easier to talk about the hurtful emotions and thoughts that often lie beneath the surface. So reflect on one another's core Enneagram wound or fears from the following list.

Type	Belief of What Brings Attachment	Corresponding Core Fear
One	Being good	If I am not all good, I am all bad and not worthy of love.
Two	Helpfulness	If I am not serving or being served, I am not worthy.
Three	Achievement	If I am not gloriously achieving, I am nothing.
Four	Uniqueness	If I am not better or unique, I am despised and not special.
Five	Wisdom	If I am not fully competent to help others, I will be overwhelmed and lose my life and attachments.

Type	Belief of What Brings Attachment	Corresponding Core Fear
Six	Loyalty	If I am not prepared, I will lose all my relational security.
Seven	Positivity	If I am not free, I will be overwhelmed and in unbearable pain alone.
Eight	Protection	If I am vulnerable, I will be overtaken and completely defeated in my heart space.
Nine	Peacekeeping	If I do not keep the peace, I will lose my relationships and disappear.

Check In Together

Whether or not you've intentionally contributed to your partner's core wounds, let your partner tell you how they're feeling as they read their type's core issues. Don't force anything on them. Let them vent a bit about how their growing-up years or life together with you have possibly contributed. Take deep breaths and try to stay connected emotionally as they're sharing. As you talk about these deeper topics together, it's important that both of you follow this acronym for "attune"—coined by Dr. John Gottman's former graduate student Dan Yashimoto—to stay healthily attuned to your conversations.

- **A**wareness
- **T**urning toward them
- **T**olerating different opinions
- **U**nderstanding versus agreeing
- **N**on-defensive listening
- **E**mpathy[2]

If you're sensitive about attachment wounds, remember that almost every relationship has them at some point. If not at the beginning, then sometime across a span of time, couples inevitably have issues to work through. In any case, knowing the label of attachment injury is less important than knowing how to get through and move on when one such injury occurs.

You may be wondering why you have to address attachment issues at all. Can't people just suck it up when someone offends them? (The more aggressive stances—Three, Seven, and Eight—may especially be wondering about this since they tend to move on *too* quickly sometimes.)

While we should always try our best to be positive, the injuries are more severe and not quite as simply managed as offering Tylenol or a pat on the back. Take my word for it, it's best not to ignore them. Though they're not seen on the surface, these attachment wounds may be the dragon in the room or family system from which everyone feels the heat. That heat is not the glow of love but the fiery flames of injustice burning and brewing inside one or both partners.

If you've had one or more of these issues in the past and they are truly already healed, don't rush in with worry or the sense of having to rehash them all over again. God offers grace, as we are reminded in Psalm 103:12, and we must follow suit with ourselves and others, as there *will* be hurts along the way. But as Tolkien said, we can grow deeper in love after grief joins us: "Though in all lands love is now mingled with grief, it grows perhaps the greater."[3]

If you do sense you need to heal an attachment wound, keep this in mind: Just as we all love differently, so do we all heal differently. You will need to work with one another on what feels the safest to you. It may take a few tries, but with some patience, love, and deep breaths, you'll get there!

Variety in Healing Experiences

As you move through healing together, remember that even individuals of the same type may differ in the healing process. For instance, some individuals who identify as a One will want a declarative logical statement of repentance and not feel at all safe in the emotional realm. Another One will feel that words are mere lip service and repel them in favor of a much deeper healing experience. Still another One may want physical touch or feel that someone working hard to make extra income is the best way to show sorrow. These nuances and exchanges of healing may also mirror male and female norms and cultural norms in addition to personality type differences.

Below is a specific way many people have healed together in my practice as I've done some of my own marriage healing. You can try to heal attachment wounds together in private, but if that doesn't seem to work, I highly recommend working with a safe third-party individual who can help remind you to breathe and to otherwise regulate your emotions. *You're not a failure if you need this support.* It just means the third party is trained in knowing how to slow you down, is paying attention to your nonverbal language, is supporting you empathically, and can allow you the accountability and space to push through your defenses to access those hard-to-reach emotions.

A Couple's Attachment Wound Healing Practice

Give yourself about an hour to work on healing a wound together. Some people will process issues in less than an hour, but this is the average amount of time to allow for issues to be explored with reasonable recovery. Below are several steps you can take to walk through the process together.

1. Decide who will share if you're both present. It may be just one partner. If there are major issues, allow just one person

to have the floor, with plans for the next partner to take time to share the following week or month.

2. The person who is speaking will share *just one* of their attachment issues and the thoughts, feelings, or sensations that have ensued as a result of the hurt. If your spouse is sharing and needs a reminder of your love and relationship stability, make sure you create safety with words first. You may have to navigate what this means to each of you. It may be compliments or terms of endearment or the commitment to not leave. Or it may be phrases like, "This is what I observed when we experienced . . . and this is what got enacted in me . . ." or, "I was telling myself this negative story about it. Was that true?"

3. The other partner, even if they remember the event differently, must put themselves in a state of compassion. You don't have to feel the same way about yourself that your partner does in this experience, but you can support them with caring and love, remembering their core Enneagram issues and explaining your perspective also. To stay connected via heart and body during the conversation, you can take deep breaths as needed, put your hand on them, or touch foreheads a little if they're interested in touch as part of the process. Otherwise, go together on a walk and talk, stretch your body, or allow yourselves time and space to shift to get comfortable.

4. The partner who shares the attachment injury must also remember their partner's Enneagram type core issues and how their partner was trying to survive with their defense strategies, hurtful as they felt. When they have shared and talked the issue through, it's important to really distinguish if they want healing.

5. Whether you as the listening spouse feel this was an issue or not, instead of allowing defensiveness to hijack your

system, try to acknowledge the courage it took to address the issue your spouse brought up. Validate your deep love and commitment to them. Whether the wound was intentional or not, it mattered to one of you. Your mutual desire to glow together as brightly and with as much depth and rootedness as possible requires this kind of validation.

6. As the listening partner, help your spouse to feel your authenticity as you apologize for any attachment wounds you have been a part of for them. Be careful not to take blame for something you did not do.

7. As the partner asking for healing, don't forget compromise is always in order when we heal with another person who is also at least slightly broken by life's experiences. Thank your partner for the courage it took to try to bridge this gap.

8. If it's comfortable to gaze at one another, allow for some sadness and vulnerability to show, such as serious faces and tears. Remember, if it feels better to walk and talk while you do this, that's okay! Hold hands or show some form of soothing, soft tonality as you address your partner with compassion and closeness. Decide together what constitutes closeness since all spouses are unique here.

9. Consider exploring your spouse's apology language if you have walked through this kind of thing before. Try apologizing a few times or in a few ways if necessary. This often includes a verbal apology. Don't make your spouse feel bad if they don't share your style of apology. Just take a deep breath and try to learn what they want here. Let them know that you love them deeply and want to move forward together as a team.

10. If you share a faith life together, don't forget the important step of prayer together. Do not be manipulative or rush a

spouse in prayer. Be kind, open, and as full of gratitude as possible. If you're sad, be honest about that before God. Ask God to help you be mindful of one another's gifts and to help you cast a light versus a shadow together to current and future generations in your influence. Ask God to heal the brokenness between you and the hurts of the past, as well as to bring you a brighter future together. It's helpful to remember Psalm 147:3 here: "He [God] heals the broken-hearted and binds up their wounds."

Timing Is of the Essence

Sometimes a spouse is not ready to heal. We need to remember that as strong and brave as you think your spouse is, they also have very sensitive roots many times. They may see even your well-meaning comments as threatening to their core beliefs about themselves if they are still working on things. It's helpful for a spouse in this position to be offered time to reconvene after some rest, and this time period will differ for each couple. Don't forget to ask for the help of a therapist, coach, spiritual director, or pastor as needed. Personal mental health cannot be sacrificed, nor should you be at the mercy of someone who is holding resentment against you and will not let up. Even one person can work on forgiveness practices.

One more thing: Don't bring up attachment injuries too regularly or you will exhaust your spouse. Bring major hurts up one at a time. If you have layers of hurt, spread these conversations out across a few weeks or months, depending on the season of life you're in. And don't forget to add fun in between.

Use logic and positivity along with emotion. Remember that partners must not be overly relational, overly idealistic, or overly comfort-oriented as they examine steps to healing. It is very likely that your spouse will still annoy you sometimes. It is normal to have a myriad of feelings about one another across the long days and years. Forgiveness practices are just that: practices. They are not onetime-only situations, so continue to work through the above model as issues resurface.

Most of all, dear reader, remember that healing takes time. After initiating healing together, let things settle and shift a bit. In other words, don't assume that just because the conversation didn't go exactly the way you planned, doom is your destiny. Perhaps the love shared, imperfect as it was, will make you feel lighter or stronger together merely since you addressed things. Maybe your spouse will rest or process the conversation later and then change. Types One, Eight, and Nine particularly often need time to digest and come back to a conversation later. So give it time.

As you try to heal, one of the hardest things about being vulnerable enough to ask your mate to meet an attachment need is when they miss the mark. If you're still stuck with feelings about an old attachment wound, remember to call upon support to help you through.

A Forgiveness Practice

Below is a model of forgiveness that has been vital in my life and practice over the years.

Take five or ten minutes for this exercise. You may want to include instrumental music or white noise as a backdrop for added focus or put your social media out of reach. Your body has complex defense systems that are in place to protect you and will not allow you to fully release an emotional injury unless you acknowledge the physical stress it has caused and then release that stress with intention.

You may do this exercise seated and at home. Your forgiveness work may also involve journaling, crying, sad songs, poetry, or fitness if you're someone who likes to process on the run.

1. Take deep breaths as you settle into allowing yourself to consider the hurt so your body knows you're safe. If you're actively anxious, take two breaths in followed by four breaths out using diaphragmatic breathing and anxiety tools. Your body generally will not respond well to forgiveness work or social interaction if your heart rate is more than one hundred beats per minute.

2. Focus on and actively address the situation of hurt with your spouse or another person. Along with your deep breaths, allow yourself to remember the reasons you're hurt. Notice areas of your body that feel tight or tense as you think about the wound someone caused you. Breathe through it for at least thirty seconds to really allow some time to pause.

3. Make a plan to safely address the wound so you can get deeper healing if you need to talk it out, pray, set a boundary, or seek further counsel.

4. Take a moment to open your hands and heart to God, remembering that the person you're holding offense against is a complex being who has different neural components and history than you. In other words, they have a brain and body you can't fully know and therefore cannot fully judge.

5. Take any lingering experiences of shame or grief to God and remember how beloved you are. For example: "I release [name] from my full judgment. I will set the boundaries I need in the future so I feel safe. I reflect on the reminder of how beloved I am to God." You may reflect on God's delight from Zephaniah 3:17 or on his reminders in Psalm 46:11. Dr. Curt Thompson also recommends reflecting on the imagery of a beautiful space, picturing God's delight over you,

and doing other spiritual practices that can help you work through toxic breaches of attachment.[4]

6. You now typically need time to think about something good your spouse or the other person did recently for you or others. For example, "He is a good father," or "She helps others at work with her many gifts." Be as specific as necessary to revive some positive feelings so neither you nor the other person is left in a shame space.

7. Breathe deeply a few times and release this person to God in prayer. Allow yourself to consider gratitude and to reflect on the rest of your day ahead.

The Benefits of Forgiveness

Remember, forgiveness releases the offended person from the hate and bondage of shame or rage that accompany unforgiveness. Forgiveness frees the offending person from carrying more than their due share. It allows both parties to take active steps toward tuning in together. In other words, it's a leaning in versus leaning out, giving you both a chance to connect using your God-given survival method of healthy attachment and interdependency, and to admit that, fallen as you are, you truly need one another.

When negative actions, shame, or angry feelings come up against your partner or the other person again, repeat the above steps. Visit a coach or counselor if it's particularly tough or you need deeper layers of healing with a trauma specialist.

The Lord's Prayer

You may also include specific prayers in your time of forgiveness. If you use any written prayer, make sure you're really breathing through it and focusing on forgiveness, not just absently reciting a chant and checking off a box.

I recommend incorporating the Lord's Prayer. When the followers of Christ asked him how to pray, this is the prayer he gave them.

> Our Father in heaven,
> hallowed [holy] be your name,
> your kingdom come,
> your will be done,
>   on earth as it is in heaven.
> Give us today our daily bread.
> And forgive us our debts,
>   as we also have forgiven our debtors.
> And lead us not into temptation,
>   but deliver us from the evil one.
>
>   Matthew 6:9–13

AFTERGLOW

Illuminate: When would be a good time to walk through healing a wound? Make the commitment to do this with your partner or on your own, and set dates for healing together or individually as often as needed.

Spark Up Heart-to-Heart Conversation: Which practice will you use to aid you in opening your hearts, minds, bodies, and souls together as you lean in to do this work? Remember, you will each walk through these practices a bit differently, so let things settle as they will.

Glow Brightly Together: Remember that marriage needs maintenance. How often will you check in about attachment wounds? Schedule maintenance appointments with a counselor or get agreed-upon dates on the calendar for the two of you at home.

8

Afterglow

Lighting the Path for the Journey Ahead

It is my spirit that addresses your spirit; just as if both had passed through the grave, and we stood at God's feet, equal—as we are!

CHARLOTTE BRONTË[1]

Marriage often has a lot of mysteries to decode. One such mystery in my marriage surrounds Wes's birthday. Each year he alludes to not wanting any fanfare. He does the whole "Don't make a big deal, your love is enough" speech that I'm sure you've given or been given at some point in your life. After studying the Enneagram, I've learned to decode Wes's particular "why" behind this statement. He's a type One, so it intrinsically feels wrong to spend money on himself unless there's a practical need. However, he still hopes that someone will spend money on him. After all, he's human, and it's his birthday.

Back in our early days together, I didn't know this yet. Thus, for many years I missed the chance to really spoil him. One unfortunate celebration in this time frame was when I took him to a park on his birthday in Ann Arbor, Michigan.

Ann Arbor wasn't the problem. In fact, we've always wanted the classic bumper sticker that says, "I'd rather be in Ann Arbor." You know why if you've ever been to this gorgeous city! The famous University of Michigan college town has urban forest and conservation projects everywhere, and offbeat cafés are interspersed with trendy hot spots for studying or daydreaming. The downtown aesthetic encompasses something for every personality type to enjoy.

However, we weren't going downtown. I was taking him on a surprise canoe trip in August in a remote park on the outskirts of town.

Once we got inside the canoe, I gave Wes his practical gifts: a single Hostess cupcake and a new C. S. Lewis book he had been waiting for. We had time together to just read and paddle and for him to eat his cupcake.

Yet I had forgotten a major detail. Wes's birthday falls during the hottest, murkiest, most miserable weather of the year in the northern hemisphere. But we paddled along, doing our best on the route. The sun was blazing unforgivingly directly overhead. Wes (who you now know as a five-senses body type) cringed through the sticky sunscreen application and bug spray.

We went through the motions with all the positivity we could muster. I lit his birthday candle. We read his book. We paddled around in circles. But the truth is, it was humid and muggy, and there were small flies buzzing all over our faces.

I'm giggling as I type this now, but at the time we were both just eager for that ride to be over. We eventually admitted how bad it was going and laughed as we turned in our canoe early. We got into our college beater of a car and landed at our favorite coffee shop downtown, Amer's on State Street. We read his C. S. Lewis book aloud in the cool air-conditioning with sodas and bagels.

Every time we look back on that well-intentioned celebration, we groan, but honestly, we also laugh really hard. We remember my youthful, starry-eyed idealism in thinking midday in August would work for a romantic canoe ride. We remember Wes's extreme sensitivity and resentment about body sprays and lotions, and we laugh harder yet. Still, in each of us, there was and is love through the mistakes, our personality quirks, and the hard times that often ensue from them.

Seeing my parents' love story end as their lives ended also helped me to see that even if at times we wish the ride was over, it's sad when it finally is. It's then that we see clearly. These normal, everyday events, frustrating though they are at the time, are part of real living. There is a deep joy that comes from simply attaching to our people in relationship. If we are fortunate to live long enough, there will be joy even in taking one another to yet another medical appointment in our elder years.

In other words, sharing the journey together—peaks and valleys both—is a privilege we enjoy as couples and as groups. Because let's face it, we all need each other.

As I'm coming to realize this, I'm also reminded of the fact that we need both love and light for the journey. Love is showing up for one another again and again when one or both of us are stuck in the hardest and most vulnerable spaces. Love isn't just a tit-for-tat expression of love languages or finding the perfect conflict style. It's about living a life of wonder, humor, and gratitude for even the small things we're able to do together while we are fortunate enough to have breath.

I'm not alone in drawing you toward a healthy dose of optimism, emotions, and realism. As Dr. John Gottman explains in *The Relationship Cure*, our marriages benefit so much from lightness, or a "willingness to turn toward another's sense of silliness . . .

and have a little bit of fun!"[2] Laughter and levity are some of the best secrets of happily married couples, especially around small, everyday conflicts.

As we continue this work together, let's continue putting in love and light to keep our love shining across the years. Instead of getting lost in the magnitude of constantly analyzing every little thing about our types, we must remember some days and moments are great while others are outlandishly hard. We must liberally give ourselves and one another grace and healthy perspectives as we encounter marriage mishaps.

We will have some days when we win and, even with perfect planning and loads of maturity, some days when we lose. That's okay! It's not just the big, sweeping, perfect days but the little, interesting iterations that make the most magnificent marriage over the years.

A droopy candle on a hot August day, a mountaintop experience at Beehive—in my experiences and yours, we're learning as we go.

And you know what? The healthiest couples *never* stop learning. They take breaks, rest, and repair, but they ultimately never give up on hope and faith for building a meaningful life and legacy together.

As you continue to shape an interesting life together, remember these four basic principles to continually find your greatest glow together again and again:

- **G**ive to each other and the world with your unique mission and gifts.
- **L**ove one another with intention, emotion, and lots of deep breaths.
- **O**ffer grace and compassion to yourself and each other as you repair.
- **W**elcome in laughter, fun, and learning each day.

Bookmark this page for when you need it. When it's time to pull back for a big-picture look together at your marriage, you'll have a rubric for how you can really shine across seasons and become a reservoir for one another.

Before we begin the final pieces of the journey, let's do one final exercise together: Let's refine your marriage mission. Take a moment to remember the gifts of the nine Enneagram types:

One—Goodness
Two—Love
Three—Truth
Four—Compassion
Five—Wisdom
Six—Courage
Seven—Joy
Eight—Protection
Nine—Peace

As you look at this simplified list, think about the specific gifts of you and your spouse. For example, if you're the One and Nine Glow, your basic mission is to share goodness and peace with one another and in the world. Because these are core features you each exude naturally when you're healthy, you'll almost never grow tired of at least aiming to love each other and your community outwardly. You can even decide which organizations to volunteer with or which groups you will participate in or lead for the widest scope of your glow out there!

When Storms Cover Your Glow

Remember that even with the best of intentions in marriage, clouds can cover your collective sunshine at times. Hold tight by choosing

179

to love one another in these moments even as you come apart. Pause and take deep breaths. To say marriage is hard work is a gross understatement. Yet there's something mysterious and holy about staying through the stormy seasons together and coming out on the other side with new growth and refinement.

In addition to the hard moments together, there are irreplaceable losses that inevitably take place across a marriage of potentially multiple decades. There are issues that, even if they don't cause attachment injuries, can still take you down. In these sorrows, encourage one another to laugh and love. As Solomon reminds us in Ecclesiastes 4:10, when one falls down, another picks them up. This is in reference to one another as well as your community.

When you're both down, which happens sometimes, it's important to find space where you can reach out. Friends or even strangers often come out of the metaphorical woods to take care of and minister to you in ways you never could have done on your own. Despite the stress of the world, I've seen that people really do root for love and marriages to work.

It's a hallmark of a healthy society to have healthy families. If you let safe others into your story during key moments when you need support, often they will show up because they care about you, especially if you are courageous and humble enough to share about your needs. They may show up for you in clumsy ways that don't help as much as you'd like, but knowing they care gives you an added impetus to push through the pain.

Even those of us with a love of independence are ushered into the precious vulnerability of community as grace is stirred when we need help. When others show up to rally around us, it moves our very spirits.

In seasons of hardship, it's okay to lament. One of my daughter Hannah's favorite movie quotes from A League of Their Own sums up this idea well: "It's supposed to be hard. If it wasn't hard, everyone would do it. The hard is what makes it great."[3]

Keep the Adventures Glowing

Because marriage is hard and also because it is great, I hope you continue to refresh yourself so you can make it through the long haul together. Your refreshment cannot be compromised. If you don't have your batteries charged, there's no way you can get through the challenges of life individually, together, or societally.

Start with daily self-care emotionally, physically, and spiritually. You can also think of this in terms of the self-preservation instinct. As a couple, it's best if you have at least six hours weekly of pure quality time together, including dates or adventures. I also hope you'll set aside time to plan adventures together throughout the year and to plan sexual intimacy.

Also, save time for just pure rest together. Amid the hard work of balancing your various types and triads, you absolutely must have agreed-upon ways to retreat and not overdo, as I've come to learn.

All in all, dear reader, I hope that when you encounter trouble of many kinds, the pages of this book may become a well-loved, marked-up accompaniment for your personal and relationship work across seasons. It's so important for you to share your gifts and your glow in the world, for I cannot emphasize enough that it is your unique impression together that makes a difference in a world of shadows.

There's one thing you must remember above all: to pause. A pause is a sacred gap that allows you time to balance, breathe, and consider others. It is just a moment, but in that moment, you can take an intentional breath and consider the impulses and urges of your temperament with clarity and focus.

These pauses truly lead us away from moving in the world based on our instinctive desires. They allow for our subconscious to be measured by wisdom, love, and compassion for others. They improve not only our own lives, as you can see, but also the lives of our spouses, families, and communities for better so we can show up and shine brighter together.

If you have a faith life, spend time in prayerful lament and gratitude as often as needed to remind yourself of the ways to love the people in your life. No one is perfect. We must remember the fundamental attribution error once again for ourselves and others. Instead of spreading the darkness of hate, let's bravely share from a well of grace as we lift ourselves onward with an inspiring thought from J. R. R. Tolkien: "While there's life there's hope!"[4]

AFTERGLOW

Illuminate: When can you fit in six to ten hours of time together per week to enjoy one another's company? Plan more dates and healthy adventures into your life every week and month in some way.

Spark Up Heart-to-Heart Conversation: If we're being honest, there's always more work to do. What feels like it's still undone in your life? Make a plan to work on this continual process of growing and glowing together.

Glow Brightly Together: What do you bring together to the world based on what you've discovered here and elsewhere? Advocate for more of this in your life.

The Glow Pairing Dictionary

Varying Hues in Each of the Forty-Five Pairings

Kindling in pure, powerful flame, fuses you and me in one.

Charlotte Brontë[1]

This glow pairing dictionary will help you have a generalized mini treatment plan so your glow out in the world can be as vibrant as possible across seasons. I have provided you with tips and a focused strategy of your gifts and glow together in early stages. I've also included how you may particularly encounter or pass through shadowlands as you evolve together.

I'm so excited for you to find your glow together. But before we head into your glow pairing tips, remember this: While your pull together as spouses feels almost gravitational or magnetic at times, there are other times when your relationship may feel distant or even painful. As you walk through the stages of your pairing together, you'll find that your gifts and shadows together combine in many different ways across time.

183

There are a few more important things to remember as you journey through your types together. First, no one goes through these stages in a perfectly linear direction. You may find yourself immersing in two or more stages at once. More than likely, you will go through them as a pattern many times over. If you get stuck in your relationship, I recommend starting over from the beginning stages to solidify your basic connection and getting self-care. Lament as needed. Forgive as a continual practice.

Second, do your personal growth work, celebrate your glow out in the world, and plan for grand adventures. With this basic structure in mind, you will indeed shine brighter together!

In the final stage of finding your glow, instead of simply beaming, your shared love radiates to help others as well. Couples combine together over time to shine a strong, steady, and enduring flame that impacts the world for good.

Divergence among the Forty-Five Pairs

You will not walk through the stages just like everyone else. You won't do it exactly like your friends, neighbors, or Wes and I did, even if you share our types. Each of the forty-five pairings in the Enneagram world will walk through these stages a little differently, and each person within those pairings will have even more nuance. These varieties come from instinctual sequencing, with consideration for each person's neuroplasticity, family-of-origin issues, epigenetics, culture, generation, gender, traumas, attachment wounds, mental health, and addictive patterns.

Don't Compare Your Glow across Types

This caveat is so important: *Try not to compare yourself to other pairings.* Your glow *would* be different with different partners, to be sure. As Taylor Swift says in her song "Illicit Affairs," "You showed me colors you know I can't see with anyone else."[2] However, as the song also notes, there is a darkness and loneliness that result from relationship hopping and secret rendezvous that promote fantasy and multiple romances, which aren't based on anything more than self-focused, short-term distractions from life's hardships that must inevitably be faced squarely.

Though affairs offer intensity and a short-term reward, they are not the true, lasting love that stays. They do not offer love even when skin is saggy and bones are frail. One-night stands or fantasies cannot comfort us with the love that holds faith for better days when we are hanging our heads over the toilet or crying our eyes out together. This loose anchorage cannot hold for the long journey toward a collective betterment when the relationship is merely about prowess or personal gain.

As you and your partner face your issues, it will take ongoing hard work and authenticity to shift and balance in all the ways that you will need to while your relationship takes new and refined shape across seasons. When life changes and stretches you, it's vital that you embark on creating safe terrain together for the long haul.

May your pairing's mini treatment plan across the following pages be a great road map for the shadowy times when life gets tough as well as a reminder for what healing across seasons may look like as you celebrate the shining moments.

Without further ado, now it's time to find the stages of your glow together! As you dive in and read about your pairing, don't forget to keep the following three "Afterglow" questions in mind so you can connect together and talk about the journey. May this be a reference you can enjoy and seek for guidance across the long but worthy years of life lived collectively. And in the wise words of Tolkien, "May it be a light to you in dark places, when all other lights go out."[3]

AFTERGLOW

Illuminate: What part of your glow comes from your biggest differences in the gifts you each bring? (For example: "I never would have tried public speaking, but my spouse's extroversion rubbed off on me, and now I regularly share my story in the world without much stress.")

Spark Up Heart-to-Heart Conversation: What is something important to each of you that has become important to both of you over time because of your emerging gifts? (For example: "My spouse is a Nine, and their favorite charities are environmental causes. Their glow in this area rubbed off on me, and now we both love to show up in this area in various ways.")

Glow Brightly Together: What is one area in which you will try to collectively serve your family and the world with your unique Enneagram Glow? (For example: "As a Three and a Four, we love to share our projects in the world. One of us is an artist and the other is the social media manager.")

Glow Plans for Each Pairing

Type One with a Type One

Shine: The One and One find a worthy companion in each other in their foundational quests for both self-development and world improvement. In their shared passion to help others through trials, two Ones truly shine out with hope for the betterment of the shadows of the world. In addition to their mutual justice orientation and predisposition to notice the microcosms of the world, they share a desire for goodness. Ones also share a mission to create a safe oasis for respite when the work is finally done each day.

Heal: When one of the types in this pairing forgets true fun, rest, or relaxation in their quest to improve the world, themselves, or others, the other One can help address their inner (and outer) critics with empathy and compassion, even as they understand their partner's desire for doing things exceptionally well. Ones can also help each other to think critically before saying yes.

Shadows and Throwing Shade: The inner critics run hard at both partners in this relationship. Ones will often count who does more, though this is impossible to detect, and they'll burn the wick at both ends, leaving both in the body triad feeling quite resentful. When a One finds themselves fantasizing about how others' lives or marriages seem perfect, they must remember that they don't see the inside of everyone else's relationships. A deeper delve would surely find inconsistency and imperfections. Ones should take the road less traveled and talk out conflict together. No matter how much they wish things would not take maintenance, everything worth doing does, so relationships are well worth it.

Immerse: Both partners need to take time to immerse in body-work and forgiveness and to realize that all humans are prone to the fundamental attribution error. They need to work on sensory integration with one another or an occupational therapist to see if either of them have issues to deal with related to the five senses. They do well to watch their reactions when their spouse doesn't do what they like. Both partners need to digest and think through a variety of human filters. Time and grace are needed for their loving intentions to take effect.

Glow 2.0: After they've leveled off with self-care and spousal care, they can finally administer smaller doses of correction and celebrate small wins or even partially done jobs. They will find family and friends open to them in new ways, and their own joy increases within this caring framework that does not forget compassion.

Afterglow: This pairing needs quarterly getaways, often doing something nature oriented. They can enjoy serving at church or school together and then relax in the glow of a good deed afterward. They also enjoy hosting parties together or attending some kind of adult education class like cooking.

Type One with a Type Two

Shine: The One and Two join together in their mutual desire to bring goodness and sunshine to the world. They both enjoy the finer things in life, like hospitality, beautiful decor, and peaceful settings to come home to after busy days. An energized pairing, the One and Two both work hard, and the Two does a great job of rewarding the One for all their hard work by planning many meaningful family times together.

Heal: In important early and later glow stages alike, the One can add a pivotal understanding to the Two, making sure the Two feels self-worth and dignity, which may not have always been part of their understanding. The Two can remind the One of their intrinsic worth and the importance of processing feelings, and they can become a space of fun and encouragement for the One.

Shadows and Throwing Shade: This pairing moves quickly and can lose their sense of being a couple if they don't set boundaries around their service and remember they are accepted even while at rest. Keeping themselves around a community who differs from them and sharpens them can help bring them back to reality. This community can help them find an even greater reach with not only those they serve but friends as well. As much as those they serve will be grateful, if this couple is looking for friends, they must be willing to be vulnerable about their issues. Compromise is essential for both types. Saying sorry is a practice a One must understand and admit to because feeling some grace is very helpful to a caring Two, who struggles with identity. Apologizing is easily done once pride is put aside.

Immerse: The Two must familiarize themselves with boundaries, while the One does the same (especially if they lean to a Two wing or have been married a while and the Two is rubbing off). Both also need to do daily bodywork with some independence. Since they are dependent types, doing things on their own is important.

Glow 2.0: They may stabilize and set enough boundaries to be able to make meaningful changes. They can also work on their collective shadow and make sure they don't come across as judging to their community. Taking a night out is awesome, but with the massive amounts of energy spent on pouring out to the world, quarterly trips to get the One out in nature and the Two the true attention and adoration they need are helpful. Pictures help the Two look back on those fun memories when the One returns to business.

Afterglow: Both get into a tailspin of serving even more as they dig their heels in to find affirmation from being both right and loving. The Two will do well to make sure the One feels loved by acts of service or physical touch after a date night, and the One needs to consider the Two's feelings and energy level. The Two makes the One feel honored and loved, and the One makes the Two feel served and seen.

Type One with a Type Three

Shine: Always moving, the One and Three beautifully polish one another for a lifetime of love, each encouraging the other to their maximum shine and goals. They are an achieving, fast-paced, and fun-loving pairing. Both logical, they have perfectionist tendencies as well. They deeply love one another just for who they are even as they continually strive to be their best together and individually.

Heal: Often there are major issues in the backstory of one or both partners, hence the perfectionism. It's quite helpful for one partner to help the other see both their desire to do the right things and their need for acceptance and love despite flaws. The One keeps the Three from cutting corners and shows them the ethics of doing good in the world just for the sake of goodness, not for social accolades or by deceiving or exaggerating. The Three helps the One to find the joys of braving performance and celebrating it being done well, even if it isn't quite perfect.

Shadows and Throwing Shade: This particular pairing is prone to overworking more than any other pair, as they spur one another on and also stay in their own lane working hard. They need to remember this and take regular date nights. The One will call the Three on their smoke and mirrors, but they will often forget to hold the Three accountable to real change since they themselves often run ragged or are overworked. They both need accountability to rest or they will forget to. Then the Three may self-deceive and the One may build up resentments, and both types forget the very good and real work they do. This pairing stays busy and is perfectionistic, so they may each get everything they want in terms of quality items and satisfying homes yet feel unsatisfied together emotionally.

Immerse: This pairing, while deemed most likely to suffer from busyness driving them apart, is also quite easily and logically healed. Neither typically wants to delve too deep into an abyss of illogical feelings. They can get emotional connection by taking regular date nights, getting bodywork in, and staying activated but connected. This requires both of them to believe they are worth the efforts despite their busyness and that having quality time together is the right thing to do. The One also needs to soften judgment toward the sensitive Three, who deals with shame and deceit, while the Three can offer their gifts of hope and encouragement to the One and their inner critic.

Glow 2.0: This couple moves fast. As they find their stride, it's important the Ones encourage the Threes not to wear a mask to please them. Instead, they should encourage the Three to be themselves even if they have a different system or are a bit quirky, as those quirks will endear the couple to one another across time. Since the Three basks in the adoration of the One, it is important for the One to build the Three up, even if they themselves do not particularly value this type of love language and even though the Three is less than perfect (since no one can meet the high standards of a One). It must also be noted that the One is less than ideal, as all humans are, but it is not necessary for the Three to bring up critiques, since the One is already hard on themselves. Instead, they can find ways to bring comfort and fun to the One, since a Three often has a natural proclivity for both.

Afterglow: The anxiety level of the One and the Three together rapidly rises from time to time, since their hard work and fast-moving bodies can stimulate a great amount of doing and a lack of rest. Their relationship can't play second fiddle to the One's many tasks and lists and the Three's endless goals and doing. Thus, this pairing needs to be grounded and firm in executing the regular date nights they set up together (even if they're at home) so neither is tempted to cancel them. They are in danger of putting "right" or "best" before the relationship, and this is a grave mistake. Instead, the practice of releasing stress by simply and unproductively relaxing together is both right and best and also attractive to others, who can't help but see their mutual strengths of goodness and love lived out. This pause for relationship efforts actually helps them in their mission of modeling excellence to the world.

Type One with a Type Four

Shine: The One and Four come together in early forms as an ideal expression of love, with shared values, a mutual desire for detail, and a love for what is good and right in the world. The One loves that the Four moves with order and care.

Heal: The Four helps the One by empathizing with them and understanding their inner critic quite well. The One will help the Four in their inhibitions, while the Four will help the One to feel more of their emotions and to move more slowly through the world in the sheer wonder and fun of it all.

Shadows and Throwing Shade: The Four and One both grow cold and stubborn when upset. This can last far too long if both are stuck in their ideas in judgment or they keep too busy with parallel lives. Also, the One likes to fit in while the Four likes to stand out. So the One needs to let the Four have their tastes and appreciate that they have higher-level aesthetic and artistic depths that attract others. These things may be lost on a practical One, who demands tradition and rejects the Four. The Four also needs to let the One wrangle them back toward some social norms since we do need social convention to a degree. The Four may withdraw into oblivion, shame, or addiction instead of facing life head-on.

Immerse: Time is a great healer for Fours and Ones, who tend to be very in demand. It's key for them to block off at least six to ten hours a week together for quality time, even if it's one or two hours a night at a time. This is something the One really respects, and they can shape healthy behaviors in their Four by not picking at them for much but truly encouraging them. Both types need to work on their inner lives since they have a strong inner critic. It's essential that the One addresses their inner wounds when it comes to their family of origin as well. This can be done with a therapist, in church, or in Bible studies.

Glow 2.0: Specially curated dates together allow this couple to fall in love with each other all over again, as they both enjoy time in ideal settings, take care to make themselves attractive to one another, and share their unique nuance. The Four challenges the One's very classic notions in a healthy way and allows them to continue to grow and see the unique beauty of their Four. The One helps the Four realize that they have so many great gifts to give so that they continue to share them in the world.

Afterglow: When they realize the beautiful artistry they have to contribute individually and hopefully together, this pairing can get very busy with good things. Although they may come to one another and the world with less judgmentalism and more grace, they still need to take their pacing more slowly than some other pairings for much-needed respite. As they nurture their moments of rest and take time to heal with their mutual sensory and aesthetics interests, they will enjoy quality time together for many years to come.

Type One with a Type Five

Shine: Ones and Fives are drawn to one another magnetically, and their love often rings deep, practical, and honest. There is strong attraction physically, a best friendship, and typically a shared ethical code. It is a quiet and fierce kind of love that doesn't often agree about everything but rests in the sacred bond itself, in family stability, and in predictable rhythms.

Heal: Fives and Ones share a goodness and an ethic that they espouse in the world, and they want to see their values lifted up and promoted. The Five also helps the One to just laugh and stop being so serious all the time, while the One helps the Five to believe in themselves and shows them appreciation when they dig into hard work. This pairing can be intensely opinioned and political, but over time and with more experiences with diverse populations, they can reduce strong prior judgments and lean into compassionate wisdom with healthy judgment as necessary. Their mutual, earnest desire to learn and to encourage learning in one another helps them have something to talk about as often as time allows.

Shadows and Throwing Shade: The One and Five pair are often sought out for advice, but they can have regularly mounting issues, mostly revolving around differing ideals for healthy relating in a family. The One often resents the Five for rejecting their leadership style, and their agitation may fuel the Five's already present rejection and incompetency issues. A less mature Five desires to go against the grain while a less mature One may like to be overly compliant with cultural trends. The Five shuts down in their anger, and the One then burns with resentment while the Five withdraws into some sort of self-soothing process and seeks affirmation elsewhere or self-rejects—usually both. Body-work and self-esteem exercises for both of them are of utmost importance. They need to share what is "good enough," practice gratitude (One), and learn healthy connection tools (Five) as they exchange their sometimes impossible-to-join differences for a perfectly imperfect love.

Immerse: The One and the Five are so logical that they need structures in place to connect on a regular basis. When one or both of them get distracted by a consuming project or interest, they can allow the relationship to slip away and their vices can overtake them. They do well to find shared hobbies that they can depend on or to purchase regular date night kits. They can also enjoy intellectual and spiritual conversations and create opportunities to flirt or banter, such as playing trivia or board games, dreaming up projects, or just relaxing with an occasional splurge of a delicious meal together.

Glow 2.0: The One and the Five have a gift for serving the world in practical, efficient ways with love and care, both together and individually. The world will be very blessed as they move into health so their intense mental states can relax enough to allow for serving, which is its own reward for these caring types. It's wonderful when they can truly step into mind, body, heart, and even soul care and come to the world with love. Both types enjoy the sheer wonder and delight of creation, and regular refreshment in nature or travel allows them to come back to their own space rejuvenated as they reflect on all the good work they've done together.

Afterglow: This pair is proud of their shared dreams and deep love. They don't need the world to inform them of their deeply held bond; it's just a no-nonsense part of their fabric. They are both very logical processors, and they have often been known to give excellent advice to others and to care for others. Yet they can also let off steam, have fun, and fully indulge in one another after the long days are done.

Type One with a Type Six

Shine: The One and the Six share a passionate, caring, well-executed, and smart love from their very first days together. They are very similar to one another in that they both like to do what is right and meet their challenges with logic, care, order, energy, and wisdom. It's very helpful for the One to have somebody who cares deeply about them and shows it with acts of service, which resolves some of their deepest concerns of not being aided. The Six admires the One for the surety of their body type instincts and ideals and because the One gets them moving more instinctually in a healthy way.

Heal: In terms of mental roadblocks, the One has an inner critic and the Six has an inner committee to work with. Both of these types remind the other to listen to the inner encouragers since they can each be completely overloaded with negativity. It is very important that those in this pairing continue to shape and encourage one another with positive reminders and not just an excess of worry or suggestions for change. They can be very good about affirming each other, even if not always themselves.

Shadows and Throwing Shade: The One loves to fix, and the Six is not opposed to receiving help. However, there can be an over-emphasis on the One acting as a parent by chiding the "bad" Six youngster, which can make them mutually miserable. Though they both love planning and serving, this pairing needs to find places to serve that are based not just in excessive need but in ways that bring them pleasure and use their particular gifts to help them avoid burnout.

Immerse: Instead of leaning on the One for their instructions each day, it's helpful for the Six to do their own thinking work and to stand strong in their own inner knowing. To do this, they must make a daily list they work off of and create a space to talk about their anxieties in a minimal time frame. Verbal processing, counselors, and good friends who also want to process frequently are helpful, as the One does not typically have the energy for reactive conversations, which the Six can be prone to. The One greatly needs a partner who encourages them to turn off work and stressful thinking for a while. The Six not only does this as they settle, but they often also add humor and care to the One's relaxation when they have a safe place to process.

Glow 2.0: This couple is very loving toward others and will continue to care for others long after they themselves are burned out. They also really shine out in love toward each other because the One is good at making sure that the Six is taking care of their own needs, and the Six is excellent at helping the One to feel valued, encouraged, and accepted. The Six will fight for their One to get self-care when the One is working too hard, and the One will help the Six to rise up in efficient action, not just deliberation.

Afterglow: As the One and the Six open themselves up to body, mind, heart, and spirit work, they can influence their community with great care. Their uncanny ability to plan fits well with their seemingly limitless head and body pairing. They can execute beautiful and detailed productions and events together and retreat afterward, celebrating their giving quietly. This happens after they've decided there are certain boundaries around their time together so they don't burn out. When they are well rested, they will reach out once again and selflessly give to one another and the world.

Type One with a Type Seven

Shine: The idealistic One and Seven pairing in a relationship inspire goodness, creativity, and fun in one another and their community together. They burst with ideas for creating memorable times, and they are often both natural in leadership roles. They are truly an opposites-attract pairing, as the Seven brings out the fun of a type One, and the One activates the hard work of a type Seven.

Heal: The One helps the Seven to unlock the inner potential that they've probably been afraid to slow down enough to access. The Seven can give the freedom, fun, and autonomy that a type One deeply desires but can almost never attain on their own since they tend to see what is missing versus what is good. Sevens do just the opposite.

Shadows and Throwing Shade: The Seven often seems to thrive in chaos, while the One despairs of it. Since the Seven tends to keep work stress and negativity private, the One thinks they have an easy life. Even if the Seven rationalizes away any deeper feelings of hurt, when the One speaks harshly to them out of annoyance, the Seven begins to resent them right back. The One likes setting up plans that make them feel good and right while the Seven wants to feel safe, which for them looks like self-care and freedom amid life's responsibilities. When their ideals are opposed, the stalemate can be long and painful. Their fast pace together can also be exhausting for one or both across time and seasons and as more people come to depend on their goodness and joy in public realms.

Immerse: The One and Seven have to realize that doing good and having fun in the world are great, but emotional processing, rest, and margin are likewise important. The Seven does this work on approaching their virtue of sobriety so they don't add too much to their plate, and underlying emotions are released. The One works on curbing their harsh judgments as they see the more honest and vulnerable heart of the Seven. They both have to learn to agree to disagree about whose needs are more important when the fundamental attribution error takes over and they both get judgmental. Compromise, seeing one another's hurts, and taking turns are better solutions. Each of them also does well to have good friends who understand them and their needs even when their spouse does not, as well as a marriage helper if the issues cannot find compromise. Since the One gets stressed often, it's very important for them to get away on budgeted vacations, family fun nights, and date nights often so they can release all the stress they carry.

Glow 2.0: When the Seven has dealt with their anxious overdoing with some healthy self-soothing tools and the One has started to rest, slow down, and quiet the inner critic, they do a good job of refining where they serve, who they serve, and how they serve, leaving resources and time for replenishment and connection.

Afterglow: The One and Seven together cast a purposeful and deeply joyful mark on the world. Because they're both idealists and have high energy, many of their dreams are realized independently and together, and there is much to celebrate and to share enthusiastically with others as they spread their joy and goodness around the world and internally as well.

Type One with a Type Eight

Shine: The One-Eight dynamic brings strength, determination, and a strong foundation of family values and social justice to the world. As two people who largely read the world through the five senses before thinking or feeling, they bring a fascinating, sheer physicality to the world that is rarely rivaled. They also healthily challenge one another in their subtle differences and allow one another's frustrations to be heard with order. They have a healthy respect for social order and care. They truly create a glow that focuses on teaching and helping others do what is good and fair.

Heal: An Eight is strong enough to help with the heavy load of a One, who feels like they've had to take care of everybody else. It is wonderful to have somebody that they can lean on for support. The One is excellent at supporting the Eight in making sure that they have boundaries and balance in their life.

Shadows and Throwing Shade: This can be an extremely busy pairing, so self-care is constantly getting off-balance as they take on more and more in the world. They both love to be autonomous, and they can be resentful if the other party tries to overly help them or parent them. This overreaching of both at times can get in the way of them being able to relax and rest at home together. Either can withdraw in vengeance or anger without solving their problems and get very stubborn or stuck in their own way of seeing the world.

Immerse: It's very important for this pairing to have a third-party helper or a humbling experience in life to soften them because they each have such strong judgments and grandiosity about their own perfection. When they realize that God holds both grace and justice, they have a new humility and softening. Bodywork helps tremendously, and talking activates their thought life.

Glow 2.0: A couple who understands that it is right and good to take care of their relationship will carve that time out. This pairing needs to force themselves to take time together to rest, to play, and to be intimate since they don't save enough time for one another. Time together just relaxing and replenishing is right and good and a base from which love and affection can shine.

Afterglow: As an Eight and a One come together, they will love the fact that when they take care of their relationship, the goodness of what they do in the world spreads to the community as well. People greatly admire their union when they can each play fairly and lean into one another's ideals and strength with positivity, not just autonomy. They need regular date nights every week as well as regular vacations where they let off steam and all that big energy.

Type One with a Type Nine

Shine: The One-Nine pair combines to exude fairness, goodness, peace, and practicality. Since both experience the world largely through body instincts, they understand one another's desire for autonomy and justice. A One will serve a Nine with a belief in holding them accountable to do hard things, which is a refreshing and awakening challenge to the Nine. A Nine often serves a One with a thoughtfulness and consideration the One has never received from anybody else.

Heal: The One does a great job of helping the Nine to see that they are worthy of stepping actively into the world with their gifts. The One sees the real potential and gifts of the Nine, and the Nine can soothe the inner critic of the One like no other. The Nine also allows the One to rest after they've been working so hard and even joins the One, who enjoys time relaxing with them.

Shadows and Throwing Shade: A healthy One understands that work will never be done until the day they die, so their endless to-do lists must have their end. When they overdo and forget this, increasing their resentment, they can expect their Nine to become stubborn or quietly resentful if they feel overtasked. Then there is a deep sense of rage that the One feels but does not speak. This can also be the case with the Nine, who avoids conflict but also feels anger intensely. If the One and the Nine don't talk about their frustrations, both can withdraw and the experience can go on for days, with both of them semi-functioning in a state of anger or annoyance, actively or passively waiting for a detonation of some sort.

Immerse: A One and a Nine may need a third party to help them see that they can have more than one perspective if judgments are high. They also may need permission to balance doing and resting, as the One's inner critic may have convinced the Nine that both of them must stay moving at all times, to the misery of both. It's very important they learn that there's a lot more to life than just comfort and incessant motion. They need to be taught that their hard work will actually have much better longevity if they take rest time. Typically, somewhere between two to three and a half hours a day for rest is a good gauge for most people, though in seasons with young children, they may need to take shifts and to have Sabbath time on one longer day a week.

Glow 2.0: Now that there is less energy and time spent on overworking, slothfulness, or judging one another, this couple has ample time to serve and relax in group and community settings that they both enjoy. It's worth it for them to have conversations about which groups they both like because some of their ideals will not be the same. They need some autonomy as well as spaces together.

Afterglow: As a Nine and a One rest, work, and serve, they must continue committing not only to personal rest but to regular and unbroken time together for lighter events—date nights, dinners, and walks—to balance their justice orientation. They also need time apart since both of them seek autonomy, even if they feel guilty asking for it. It's very important for them to pace themselves and connect in relaxed and fun ways together daily as they share their peace, justice, and goodness with the world.

Type Two with a Type Two

Shine: The huge-hearted pairing of Twos makes for a fun-loving and warm combination of deeply connected love. This pairing does not often tire of spending time together and can have hours and hours of content and sacred nurturing together.

Heal: Twos heal one another by being able to talk about the things that matter on a deep level and to nurture the other in a way that many people haven't been able to. Somebody who is intuitive doesn't always get met with this gift, and it's great for them to see it in one another.

Shadows and Throwing Shade: When life gets busy and they feel cut off from one another, they can unintentionally find their approval or seek attention from other people, especially leaders or those they feel need their especial help. As their minds develop, they may have disagreements sometimes, though they may not under-stand that that's okay. Healthy couples are allowed to disagree, to have separate interests, and to have a lack of codependency but must also have good boundaries. Both Twos should keep showing up with courage as they find self-esteem and self-efficacy within their spiritual lives, and also with healthy accountability if they are tempted in terms of fidelity.

Immerse: It's important to notice who is pursuing and who is distancing and to make sure both parties get lavished with attention and respect as they interchange these roles. It's also important for Twos to stop manipulating and directly address what's hurting them. It's helpful to add in an element of bodywork as well as spirituality so that they can lean on God when their spouse inevitably disappoints them.

Glow 2.0: As the Two learns that disappointments are part of life, they can recover well by spending time in gratitude and remembering that God has entrusted them with care and also an allowance of rest while others serve. Their gratitude stems not from a prideful belief that they are better than others but because they are aware that all good gifts come from God, including their many blessings. Often Twos in the early glow stages think that they have to present themselves as perfect helpers in order to be loved, but as they hit this stage, they understand all of humanity's brokenness more acutely and see that God's grace is the biggest part of it all.

Afterglow: The Twos realize they are allowed to take breaks, process their own feelings, and sit with one another long enough to take turns sharing their hearts regularly. They know how to take breaks just for rest and for enjoying one another's company with plenty of quality time and cuddles. It's wonderful for them to take time out of their week without cell phones on a date together, just enjoying each other's company through and through with goodies, snacks, and whatever else makes them feel happy and attuned.

Type Two with a Type Three

Shine: This affirming and extroverted pairing truly adores time together. They deeply value one another's gifts and worth with sincerity and joy. Theirs is a beautiful, vibrant love that is displayed with gusto in the world as they cheer for one another. The many gifts of this heart center pairing often merge to form a model of love to others.

Heal: The Three helps the Two set goals for themselves, not just for others, and gives them the permission they need to take time for themselves. The Two helps the Three to be loved not just for what they do but for who they are underneath. Often in their formative years, neither felt this kind of deep, natural love. It is thus very healing for them to find a validation of worth in one another, both in early stages and later stages in marriage, in many fun and challenging seasons alike.

Shadows and Throwing Shade: It can be very difficult for this pairing to have healthy boundaries around other relationships. When things get tough, they can be tempted to take cues for affirmation from others outside the marriage. If they don't take time to invest in one another's sorrows instead of looking outward for endless affirmations, they may have affairs. They may otherwise have such busy lives that they isolate themselves from one another in their madness to find accolades.

Immerse: This pair must learn how to give one another the attention they each need as well as how to love the rest of their community with humility, not vanity or pride. A relationship with God really helps them to step outside of themselves and their inner codependence. They also need to set boundaries with outside parties, to address and treat addictions, and to expose and work through deceitful behaviors they have often both covered. Therapy and support are helpful here, especially with others they trust and respect and who have healthy boundaries.

Glow 2.0: This pairing not only has the capacity to spend the recommended six to ten hours a week together, but they may enjoy twenty to thirty hours or more. Being in community with the person they love the most is a great blessing to them as they get healthy. They have open access to the other's heart when they have a relationship they can trust. They may both need regular accountability in taking on too much, and it's important that they find a space to talk about their goals with boundaries and learn how to activate their minds.

Afterglow: The Two-Three couple really enjoys basking in the love of each other on a daily basis. Though love languages or love styles will vary, this pair will enjoy physical intimacy, going on long walks, setting aside time for family, going on vacations, and celebrating big and beautiful things after the hard work is done. They will help one another to enjoy life with mutual pleasures and serve all who know them from their massive outpouring of love and light.

Type Two with a Type Four

Shine: This unreservedly, indulgently romantic Two-Four pairing offers both potential energy and kinetic energy to one another in tandem. This tenderly devoted couple balances one another in their gifts of extroversion and healing, contemplative love. Both the Two and the Four love to dote on one another as well as to be doted on. They are each happy to divulge feelings to one another that they have not been able to share safely with anyone else in their rush to care for the world.

Heal: The Four can heal the Two by allowing them to withdraw and to lean into their introverting a little bit by their own model. The Two can, with the help of the Four, slow down to take time for critical thinking and become aware of their own deeper-lying feelings with the help of the compassionate Four. The Two can get the Four moving in their body center and caring for others in a way that will help the Four to be less self-focused and more

206

action-oriented. The Two also helps to value and validate the Four and their worth by encouraging them and bringing positivity. The Four brings slowing and a sense of wisdom to the Two, who has spent their life running for others.

Shadows and Throwing Shade: Because both of these partners like to be doted on, it can be difficult for either of them to step out and nurture the other as much as they would like. The Four will retreat to consider their own feelings and wounds as their ideals come crashing down. They may not share the things that the Two knows they're feeling but not talking about, and both are silent about the inner recesses of the heart. The Two will find others to validate them in the shadow of the Four's tendency toward icy withdrawal.

Immerse: The Two and the Four have to address the fact that they both can easily manipulate many in society in order to get their needs met, and they have to decide what they want more: their relationship to be healed or the surface-level success and approval of the world. The Four will also have to decide to find gratitude for what already is versus what is lacking and to overcome jealousy that arises. One or both may need to work on leaving behind addictive or pleasurable sensations long enough to simply be strong and take on full, adult maturity. Bodywork, emotional work, and spiritual work are of the essence, as is healthy accountability with those who can call them to the carpet with love, strength, and care as they grow.

Glow 2.0: As the Two and the Four become better about facing their own problems independently and together, it frees them up to serve together in the world. They can continue to set good boundaries so that other couples who may want to infringe upon their marriage will not be able to. They realize the beautiful gifts they have in one another are enough, along with the love of God and their family.

Afterglow: This pairing is quite creative, so it's wonderful to see them move into the world with artistry. The Two may never have felt the permission to step into their life as an artist and not just an object, and the Four can remind them of this beautiful space within that can be shared with others or just enjoyed for their own creative outlet. The Two will also more naturally give the Four time to enjoy their own creative rhythms quietly. It's fun when they can team up on a project together that displays the creativity, love, and compassion of God and humans.

Type Two with a Type Five

Shine: The Two and Five join as one of the strongest opposite-attraction pairings, each symbolizing important human tenets: the need for both giving and resting well, and the need for healthy thinking (Five) and feeling (Two). The magnetic joining of these opposing dynamics is fascinating to behold. They bring a balance of warmth and wisdom to the world with their playful dance of pursuing and distancing. In time, the Two learns to show some healthy distancing self-control to the Five's earliest pursuits, and the Five will take their resolve as a puzzle and a challenge to solve. It's a thrilling, reviving dance of romance that can "rinse and repeat" throughout the relationship.

Heal: This couple allows each other to be seen as valued (Two) and valuable in the world (Five). They often add a beautiful balance of introversion and extroversion and enjoy a lot of one-to-one quiet time in their simple pleasures of doing life together in harmony and with care.

Shadows and Throwing Shade: The Two may have the "never enough" attitude, wanting more and more from the Five and to be part of every aspect of their life. This rubs against a Five, who enjoys creating compartments for relationships in their lives. Though the other relationships may only be cerebral, the Two can feel jealous. Similarly, a Five can be quite jealous of the Two, who is often out with others, which makes them feel rejected. The couple needs to see these patterns at play and talk about their rejection and ways to feel safe and mutually respected.

Immerse: As they both work on their vices and virtues, the Two realizes on a deeper level that their partner is helping them to have balance and boundaries. The Five realizes the synergy that comes from relating to others in the world and how their Two helps them to do this well. The Two also finds safe others to spend time with and activities that do not use the family's resources. The Five learns to move in the body and heart spaces more instead of just leading with the head.

Glow 2.0: This deeply relational pair can thrive, as the Five will be endlessly enamored by the Two if the Two can maintain some autonomy and warmth and respect the privacy of the Five. They also balance appropriate times for the Two to meet more social needs and the Five to stay home for R and R (rest and research). They refine their community involvement so they don't say yes too often. However, when it's a great fit for both, they do say a happy yes to either helping or participating in social events.

Afterglow: The Two and Five now have a genuine respect and appreciation for their differences but also trust one another to not push too hard for change. They desire to spend time doing what they each feel made to do in their own ways, which is to care for others, and they truly enjoy collective giving. They also often take little getaways together a couple of times a year so they can enjoy nature and the beauty of the world and their love.

Type Two with a Type Six

Shine: The Two and the Six find in one another a safe harbor of love and wisdom. They love both serving and enjoying an oasis of comfort. They share a desire to do what is right and good in the world, and they long for a safe and caring community in one another.

Heal: The Six heals many of the core wounds of the Two, who often feels like they don't get to rest. As the Six spends a good deal of time resting and recovering from the perceived bruises in the world, the Two learns they too can retreat. The Six builds up the mind of the Two by getting them thinking critically, and the Two helps the Six with their positive outlook. The Two heals the Six further by helping them to feel reasonably safe in the world and to assume better of people. Their sunshine nature and energy keeps the Six from sarcasm and fear.

Shadows and Throwing Shade: The Six does not appreciate the overgiving of the Two that may often occur without the forethought of time or a budget. The Six also may get upset with the Two portraying themselves as an attractive object on social media or in the world, in fear that they will not be faithful. The Two doesn't understand that the Six deals with paranoia and does not appreciate that the Six keeps them from serving, since the Two's giving is in direct conflict with their own feelings of worthlessness when they're at rest. This couple can both get very jealous if they feel slighted by the other.

Immerse: The Two and the Six need to do a lot of individual work to reduce codependency. They are both likely to listen to authority figures, so a counselor can help. However, they also must try to find trust in themselves and focus on the good of each other, not just the negatives, since they truly do bring one another into some balance. The Six must try to do less negative storytelling about the Two and what could happen, instead allowing in a positive mindset and trusting themselves. The Two must lavish the Six with kindness and accept humility and the grace of God, not look for the Six or the world to lavish them with validation at all times.

Glow 2.0: When the Two and Six are healthy, they can enjoy more dates and spend more relaxed quiet times together because they are doing their individual work and now have boundaries. Their glow is bright and full of fun and care, and they are romantic and able to express love. When they break the toxic codependency cycle, they are each empowered to be honest, strong, and loving.

Afterglow: The Six loves to use their planning gifts to assist with schedules and to balance out the busy life of the Two as they once again extend their care into the world. The Two gets to do the serving they love, but it's no longer out of the desire for self-esteem, since their spiritual and self-care practices help to fulfill this aspect. Meanwhile, the Six is building them up and doing way less negative storytelling about them. They both take time to think about things before saying a much-too-fast yes (Two) or no (Six) as they step into life, balance, and rest on an ongoing basis.

Type Two with a Type Seven

Shine: The Two and Seven join in a relationship as a vibrant and extroverted pairing, bursting with positivity, fun, laughter, sociability, and delicious energy. They mutually charm one another and those in their presence with a genuine mirth and exuberance rarely matched. The bright glow of these two positivity types allows them to enjoy many fun, busy activities together as they light up the world.

211

Heal: The Two and the Seven bring encouragement to one another at the early stages of a relationship as well as in ongoing moments of health. The Two is entrusted with listening to the deep fears of the Seven, which are very difficult for others to access. They have an ability to draw the Seven out safely in a way that makes the Seven feel cared about. The Seven helps the Two strengthen their mind in a way that will satisfy them both on a deeper level mentally. The Seven also validates the Two's inner worth and allows the Two to rest and indulge in the comforts of life with fun and joy.

Shadows and Throwing Shade: The Two and the Seven can be so positive that both are afraid to be honest. In their vices, they can lead parallel, happy lives of each doing their own things in order to keep getting global affirmations, only tending to one another's needs in fast, sloppy ways. Authentic love can also be hard to experience if there is lopsided praise or attention going to one or the other, as both spouses need a great deal of affirmation. Collectively they can get cliquey if someone else isn't as naturally fun or as positive and interesting to one or both of them.

Immerse: When the Two and Seven are doing their work, either with a third party or together with weekly meetings to discuss their relationship from a wider lens, they do well to integrate not only positivity but also logic, talking conflicts out calmly. They must also stop long enough in their incessant doing habits to address the deeper emotional needs of one another with specificity and care, modeling safety, compassion, and love to one another. The Two must realize the Seven has anxiety that is hard to name and give space for self-soothing. The Seven must slow down long enough to both connect with and find solace in their Two, as well as to align their futuristic vision with the Two's family-oriented heart.

Glow 2.0: When the Two and Seven have done this slowing down and addressed the harder feelings with thoughtful alignment, the world feels their care on a much deeper and richer level. They are able to say healthy yeses and nos. They also learn that quiet pleasures that don't exhaust or complicate things are very worthy. They can give one another space as they work to connect their heart and head centers instead of just speeding past one another with extroversion.

Afterglow: The Two and Seven often decide to do projects together that are mutually satisfying once they're working well in tandem. They can mentor youth with their energized glow, and they're content in their daily wonder and positivity, both pouring out and resting well together in a beautiful glow of love and light. They expand with compassion in time, reaching even people who are different with love.

Type Two with a Type Eight

Shine: The Two and Eight come together as a deeply romantic, sweeping love affair. They usually fall in love fast and hard and often quickly decide that they will enjoy a lifetime of powerful and sensual love together. Combining the practicality and vibrancy of the Eight with the open-hearted feelings orientation of the Two draws the couple together in a vivid hue that bleeds a model of pure vitality to others who can't help but see their passion.

Heal: The Eight helps the Two see their worth and shine out in their helping gifts. They also protect them from getting taken advantage of in a world that doesn't always respect their heart. The Two helps the Eight to access their own vulnerable heart in order to reach deeper dimensions of their often dormant genuine care and love for the less fortunate.

Shadows and Throwing Shade: When the Eight comes on strong and abrupt with what they see as a corrective or right lens, it hurts the feelings of the Two, who in most cases is only trying to help. When this gap in attachment occurs, the Two may try to seek identity and purpose in serving others outside the Eight's domain. This flimsy resolution will only further exacerbate whatever the conflict was. The Eight, also very sensitive and caring, may cover their pain with vengeful acts. They may go elsewhere to find affirmation of their ability to connect, causing mutual jealousy flare-ups. This passionate and giving pair can become brooding and even dangerous together with both acting out of a desire for revenge.

Immerse: Instead of just being infatuated with one another and grasping to avoid rejection feelings, both parties must understand and implement boundaries, self-care, healthy short-term withdrawing, and reflecting on their partner's perspective. Therapy or coaching is helpful here, as they are often both in need of verbal processing. They must learn to pause and reflect instead of lashing out in desperation. Part of their self-care must also be bodywork so they can release pent-up angst.

Glow 2.0: Having done their own work, this passionate pair can now focus on areas of marital boundaries, taking care to protect their relationship. In addition, it's important for them to incorporate positive storytelling about each other versus manipulating or violating boundaries. In other words, they should take turns with their dream projects and desires, keep learning how to love one another and make the other's sensitive heart feel safe, and get marriage training as needed to learn about active listening and other ways to keep partner respect and self-respect alive. They can also enjoy weekly, fun date activities together and with their family to dispel negative energy.

Afterglow: This pairing can now settle down enough to realize that there is power in both acting and not overreacting. In time they will learn there is much to say about dignified presence and quieter passion together, and they will enjoy quiet times at homes in the beautiful, comfortable spaces they create together. They will schedule getaways, be part of fun events together (though not always leading), and mentor other couples as they grow wise. After all the social times, they can fall into one another's arms with deeper trust for attuned, deeply intimate sexual pleasures or sweet rest.

Type Two with a Type Nine

Shine: The Two and Nine affirm one another's worth in mind, body, and heart as two of the most considerate types in the world. The Nine particularly encourages their ultra-busy Two to take much-needed, regular rests from their incessant pace. In this they model the body type in saying "no," even if just in quiet decline of the Two's usual "yes." The Two in turn loves to show the Nine their thoughtfulness by anticipating needs that the Nine doesn't normally ask others to meet. They join together in their favorite positive pleasures of comfort after long days, where both have typically been giving or even overgiving.

Heal: In time, the Two helps the Nine to approach their needs with presence and to affirm their gifts so the Nine can begin to work in the spaces they are passionate about. The Two often enjoys being led by someone who is good and who has wisdom to share, and this too empowers the Nine to rise up in their gifts. The Nine merges with the often unseen needs of the Two and thoughtfully tends to them in a humble way the Two has rarely seen. It is a lovely thing to validate the worth of both as they begin to heal and continue to do so throughout their marriage.

Shadows and Throwing Shade: The Two can attempt to manipulate the Nine in ways that the Nine can easily subvert or sense.

215

Sometimes the Nine will go along absent-mindedly or passive-aggressively, but if they don't want to do something, they will become stubborn or forget to follow up on formerly agreed-upon plans. It's important that the Nine speak directly, but often they don't feel that the relationship will be maintained if they do. The Two seems to confirm this as they may temporarily leave or get hysterical if the Nine doesn't do what they say they need. However, the Two must consider the fact that to be truly loved, one has to have some autonomy and be able to want to love without being manipulated. The Nine must also recognize when they are going into comfort too much and forgetting that even though conflict may temporarily create dissonance, it will ultimately bring them and the Two together well.

Immerse: The Two must find their worth even in rest or when not on display as a helper, just as the Nine must remember their own feelings are valid, even if it makes them uncomfortable to admit to having needs and emotions. They both benefit from seeing a couples helper who will assist them in finding their feelings and needs, since they are so focused on meeting the needs of others. As they immerse themselves in their work, they can start to notice when they tell themselves negative stories about why their spouse is thinking or feeling a certain way when they don't know the reason behind the story. They do well to set weekly time aside to talk about their relationship and to bring fun and structure into it as well. Compromise will be a major theme as the Nine finds their own needs and preferences and the Two learns to lean into the Nine's often comfortable plans for them instead of their wildly busy pace.

Glow 2.0: As the Nine wakes up and finds time to help a cause they are passionate about, the Two is eager to come alongside to help in any way. Indeed, when the Two finds that the Nine is awake, they actually don't mind being led a little more actively, and they often look up to the Nine and their leadership gifts. The Nine does well to value their own precious leadership gifts as well.

Afterglow: Planning for fun times together in the afterglow of serving others is not usually a problem for this pairing once they learn boundaries. Though they are naturally inclined to serve, they're also quite happy to rest and enjoy one another's company when the long days are done. It is important that they take special date nights weekly with each other and at times with other couples, as well as no-stress date days just to talk about the things they want to. They should schedule six to ten hours a week at minimum to merely enjoy one another's company while the cell phones or other parties needing help are away or asleep.

Type Three with a Type Three

Shine: Two Threes enjoy a foundation of championing one another with their huge hearts and loads of productive energy. There's room for both of them to get decent time in the limelight as well as to practice not being center stage all the time. They love affirmation and attention from each other as well as launching out together in the world as they lift one another up for all to see.

Heal: This couple can be intentional about valuing one another outside of just the work they do, and this is quite a healing experience for each of them. Because they're the same Enneagram type, they can also pick out each other's issues and flaws and learn about themselves as they see this reflection, especially their shared defense mechanism of identification. They dig in to work on their issues and help to carefully excavate and label their own feelings under all the weight of caring for the hearts of others.

Shadows and Throwing Shade: Because both Threes are found along the continuum of the inner triangle of the Enneagram, they relate not only as Threes but in the Three, Six, and Nine spaces. It's so important for this couple to realize that they are going to lack momentum sometimes, since all three of these types are asleep to their core motivations. To come face-to-face with themselves, they must do some work. With their often major codependency leanings and deeply held shame, it's also important that they meet with God on a spiritual level.

Immerse: Threes need to remember that while they're very charming and good at starting a relationship, working on maintaining one is a challenge. This is healthy for them to know so that they can explore their fast-paced, anxious mind that tends toward deceit and their often deeply seated self-esteem issues. As they dip down into growth, it's important that they take time to rest and self-soothe, both alone and with their mate, so they can get to know themselves and what keeps them calm and stable. These ambitious Threes also do well to take date nights that don't incorporate any projects, sometimes just to remind themselves that they're each loved for more than what they do.

Glow 2.0: A Three-Three couple who understands that they are more than what they do *and* that they're beloved just because they're human shines gloriously. They love laughter and downtime, and they can celebrate accomplishments well together without fear of being unknown or judged for what they do. Their dates can be relaxed, fun, and connective, authentic spaces.

Afterglow: It's lovely to see Threes winding down and having fun after the hard work has been put away and it's time again for comfort and cuddles. They love to be competitive with flirting and games, and they balance one another with a love for learning and by taking inventory of their individual mind-body-heart-soul personal wellness each week, including rest. They also do well to have a weekly check-in that has elements of planning for the relationship and to share these learnings and other gifts with those in need.

Type Three with a Type Four

Shine: The huge hearts of a Three and a Four come together in great love, support, and style. The Three helps the Four to see their beautiful gifts more clearly and step out into the world with confidence. The Four helps the Three to understand that they too have unique gifts and that they are deeply loved and regarded even while at rest. They both cherish time together after long days.

Heal: The Three works very hard to find people who will give them time and attention, and the Four wants nothing more than to collectively enjoy time and attention with their Three. It's a very beautiful pairing in this way because they love doting on one another and validating their intrinsic worth. This lovely dynamic of a future-thinking goal getter and an artistic dreamer who likes to take their time allows the couple the healing and momentum they need. When their compassion and ambition are combined, many are touched by their soothing and soulful dynamics.

Shadows and Throwing Shade: Because both parties desire a lot of attention, getting their felt needs met can take a long time. The Four can get very jealous of the Three getting attention at work, and the Three is jealous of the ways their Four draws in others without trying. Because the Four often withdraws in their envy, the Three is left in shame and sadness and will do whatever they need to cover those feelings, including lie. With both the Three's and the Four's potential for codependency, it's very important that they make their mental wellness a prioritized need. They do well to find a helper who will not be taken in by their heart type charms but who will lovingly hold them accountable to be their best.

Immerse: As the Three and Four do their self-care and mental health work, they must work through trauma with a skilled leader and learn to develop a well-balanced life that has a healthy physical, emotional, and spiritual lens so they can resist the urge to discharge all their shame onto their partner. As they influence one another, the Four helps the Three to look in the past, and the Three helps the Four to find their goals and momentum. The Four also helps the Three to just listen without an agenda, while the comfort-seeking Three can help the Four come up from their melancholic doldrums.

Glow 2.0: As they stabilize and rise up to this stage, this pair exudes a bold romance. Both partners experience deep gratitude, and their display of quiet love is available for the world to see, though now without a dependency on the world's validation. This pairing cares about doing ongoing relationship work and enjoys pointing others to the love they've found in their own bond. They learn to dedicate time each day just to play and to arouse and rearouse their romance. They deeply cherish their physical, mental, and especially emotional expressions when they are brave in taking this time.

Afterglow: The Three and Four are full of depth, love, and style. In the afterglow of their growth, they are capable of making beautiful internal and external spaces where they live and retreat safely together. Curating an inviting holding space for themselves, their family, and their guests helps them to also curate a comfortable and fun environment for their dreams to unfold. From this space of healthy introspection and support, they both dream, rest, and carry out action plans together daily.

Type Three with a Type Five

Shine: A Three and a Five can fuel the fires of love again and again by audaciously speaking into one another's worth and passions. A Three can move into goals more efficiently and with a lot more courage with somebody as wise as a Five backing them up. A Three is also able to give the Five respect for being such a good planner and being so thoughtful of the family.

Heal: The Five is good at listening to the Three talk about all their dreams and goals. They also help with planning so the Three can land on these goals in a detailed and focused manner. Their vast knowledge helps the Three to execute their plans with precision and detail over the long term, which results in a bigger vision. The Three loves to champion the wisdom and loyalty of their Five and expects the same in return, even if it's done more privately by their often adoring and even love-obsessed Five.

Shadows and Throwing Shade: The privacy of both parties can be intense and hurt one another. The Five wants a lot of autonomy and many cerebral relationships outside of the Three in order to feel competent. Still deeper issues can come in when the Three adds in their own new relationships of support that take over the role of the Five, who often concedes to these with low self-esteem.

Immerse: It's important for the Five to set boundaries, bravely foster romance with their Three, and remember the synergy that results from bringing themselves into union with their spouse. The Three must realize that building up their Five is the only way the Five is going to feel like moving toward them with intimacy. It is of utmost importance that the Three not try to be harsh with the Five's rejection issues.

Glow 2.0: As much as the Five doesn't want to be showcased in public, they want and need the Three to be a good listener when it comes to talking about their passion projects. Over time in marriage, the couple is likely to do many projects together, as well as many of the Three's project launches, with each new project being just as interesting and challenging as the last. The Three is very good at seeing the heart of the Five, even if they don't always understand their own heart. They each truly have the other's heart in mind as they serve one another.

Afterglow: This is a very caring couple who can give to one another as well as to others generously and without a second thought since they both have huge hearts. The Five enjoys building behind the scenes and stepping out only when certain, but they love to encourage the Three on their daring stage adventures all the same. As long as the Three remembers the wonderful private support of the Five, they can both truly celebrate their beautiful and complementary polarity and closeness.

Type Three with a Type Six

Shine: A Three and a Six have many complementary gifts as they both help one another not only to rise up with support but to forge ahead on their goals. They are great at teaming up in the world so that the voice of the Three can be strong and clear and the Six can play an important support role in a comfortable manner that will also be exciting and full of courage.

Heal: The Six helps the Three by loving them for who they are outside of just what they do. They are also dazzled and enamored by the way the Three is seen by the world. They love the Three's leadership style and the way that the Three advocates for them too. The Three also loves that the Six is good at planning because they often run ahead and need reminders of how to slow down and take care of their people. They make the Six feel safe, and the Six makes the Three feel very loved.

Shadows and Throwing Shade: Because the Three and the Six share so many similarities in wanting material comfort and success, they usually agree to allow the Three a large job that demands a lot of hours to pay for their expenses. Because the Three is running so fast and showing up so beautifully in the world, it stirs up resentment and paranoia in the Six. The Six becomes reactive, and the Three cannot manage them with their preferred logic. The anxiety of the Six and the anxiety of the Three can also stir one another up.

Immerse: This pairing needs to work on the deeper anxiety that may overtake them if the Three does not slow down and the Six does not feel supported by their spouse. As they find self-soothing techniques, they can troubleshoot together on how to find connection and heart-to-heart attunement even through the busy seasons. The Three needs to slow down and save enough energy to be a good listener when the Six has worries to dispel, but the Six must also do their bodywork and take care of their mental health versus expecting their Three to manage it all.

Glow 2.0: When they're moving in harmony, this pairing is fun to watch in the world as they blaze trails carefully and with passion. They are absolutely unstoppable in whatever goals and dreams they pursue, especially since the Six reminds the Three of home, family, and friends. The world indeed feels very loved and supported as they both open up their hearts to care.

Afterglow: It's so important for this ambitious pair to take time to purely rest and release from their swirling life of productivity. Although they may have some adventures they both enjoy, they also do well to allow more serene, fun, and relaxed times to disconnect and not work toward any goals. They also need actual date nights rather than planning or griping sessions.

Type Three with a Type Seven

Shine: Threes and Sevens come together with enthusiasm and passion as two people with a lot of love, intelligence, and vibrance to both give and receive. They are supportive and understanding of one another's goals and can truly celebrate one another for that reason. They know how exciting and fun it is to take new steps and to be their best selves together and apart.

Heal: The Three helps the Seven to achieve goals with tenacity and believes in them to the highest level. The Seven admires and looks up to the Three in their social and intuitive adeptness. They also help the Three lighten their load, laugh, and feel cared about amid all their serving of others and logical efficiency. The Three moves the Seven into the heart space to truly care deeply about others.

Shadows and Throwing Shade: Because the Seven can get lost in the cycle of overdoing, sometimes the Three can feel like they are not seen or cared about. Often the Seven does care deeply but feels anxious and doesn't like to admit it even to themselves. Life is a blur at times. The Seven also struggles with the way that the Three manipulates or dominates their collective time. They don't realize that the Three often has a lot of undetected anxiety as well and feels a need to control their secure people in order to maintain a healthy amount of attention and self-soothing.

Immerse: The Three doesn't always know what they're thinking and feeling, and the Seven is moving too fast to know how to help them. With both being future thinkers and aggressive, staying in one spot and learning ways to bring calm and soothing experiences to one another is good. They must balance bodywork, not just pleasures, as this will help dissipate anxiety even further. The Three can also feel the bulk of the financial load and, to keep the Seven happy on the surface, may move into deceit instead of discussing strains. However, the Seven is wise and can move into gluttony and self-protection quietly if they feel the Three's distrust.

Glow 2.0: When the Three and Seven are activated in health, they remember that honesty is the best policy. They need to hold a weekly strategy session, as it helps tremendously, and they can schedule in time together. It is important that their dates not be all about work. Instead, work and phones should be left behind for fun activities, dreaming dreams, and the lighter heartfelt, much-needed conversations these two can easily have when distractions and anxiety are down.

Afterglow: Because they're such vivacious types, others are often attracted to the Three and Seven in intense ways. This pairing needs to both talk about and set healthy boundaries for the relationship, as well as keep their romance and interest up. Taking trips together, advocating for one another in social spaces, and traveling to new and exotic destinations are fun ways for Threes and Sevens to span the globe with their shine.

Type Three with a Type Eight

Shine: A Three and an Eight in a relationship are a powerhouse combination. They have determination and passion and set unstoppable goals together. Their ambition and caring hearts launch and relaunch them into action, both at the beginning of their relationship and in many exciting iterations across time together.

Heal: The Eight will pave the way for the Three to achieve their goals with strength and support rarely felt by the Three. They will protect the surprisingly tender heart of a Three in a way that few have ever done before. Though in some ways the couple experiences polarity from the get-go, the Three also will fight harder than anyone ever has for the deeply sensitive Eight. They each hold a special and rare healing privilege in each other's lives, and they try not to take advantage of one another's vulnerability.

Shadows and Throwing Shade: Because the Three can often sense the sad or hurt feelings in the heart of an Eight, sometimes they think they also know why they're feeling this way. However, since they don't always have the same five-senses kind of reaction as the Eight, they are at times wrong. If they begin to manipulate before investigating what's actually going on, the Eight can get very upset. While the Three may try to micromanage or guess at what's happening, the Eight prefers direct discussions. If the Eight is too harsh with the Three, the Three grows anxious at the thought of abandonment and has the tendency to evade and to use deceit.

Immerse: In order to feel safe and vulnerable together, these strong temperaments need a therapist they not only greatly respect but who can offer them clear and logical steps for healing. The Eight needs to understand that other healthy perspectives exist outside of their often black-and-white perspective, but they must feel safe and disarmed first. Thus, finding a mentor they can trust with their heart is helpful. The Three needs to get self-care and do self-esteem work so they don't give too much of themselves away to the Eight or try to put on a mask of codependency, which will only further distance and irritate the Eight.

Glow 2.0: Once the Eight has learned to respect their partner and the Three has learned self-respect and embraced their own integrity, they can enjoy one another's company, respect one another's ideas, and build their dreams together. They can also take healthy withdrawing time apart as long as they have boundaries around new relationships and old alliances are not rekindled.

Afterglow: When an Eight and a Three build trust together, their glow shines brightly across the community and the world. They often like to do team activities to build one another up emotionally, even in public ways. They hold one another to high standards, but they are one another's absolute biggest cheerleaders, and they're willing to dedicate countless hours to their spouse and their partner goals, as well as to celebrate with a toast.

Type Three with a Type Nine

Shine: The marriage between the Three and the Nine creates many interweaving rhythms of trust and fun times together. Because they both often share an interest in serving the world with their myriad gifts in between the interchanges of comfort and fun, the firm foundation they build together is one of peace, love, and joy. This is a pairing of deeply caring individuals who can awaken one another to the goals of their lives as well as trust in the peaceful countenance of care that they build over time.

Heal: The Three is gifted in helping the Nine to find ways to set goals. They also encourage them when they see an untapped gift. They will not let the Nine slip into oblivion, and if the Nine is willing, they will find actionable support from their Three. The Three finds an equally considerate partner as their Nine helps them to pace themselves with their planning and to be considerate of others.

The Nine creates an environment of comfort and love they both can relax in after long, hard days.

Shadows and Throwing Shade: Downward spiraling together is a very real possibility in the Three and Nine pairing since both share many traits, including anxiety, sloth, and a deep sadness for not being known at the core. To counter these empty spaces inside, they can project their own issues onto one another or stuff things, and both become workaholics in some form. As the issues they're pushing down threaten to rise to the surface or actually come up, they may reach out for a new relationship or an addiction, possibly both. With the Nine lacking boundaries and the Three's ability to charm, they can avoid doing the work together and numb out to temporary pleasures.

Immerse: It's important to remember how very painful addressing conflict is for both the Three and the Nine. If they do address it, they feel like their partner may leave them. They may even have memories of this happening in the past. Both partners do well to have a marriage support team, pastor, or friend who can encourage them to be brave and courageous to speak the truth in love. They also need to practice staying for hard conversations and being direct about their needs. As they heal, they also need fun together, and this is a pairing who does well to spend a lot of time with each other as they commit to the work.

Glow 2.0: The Three and the Nine naturally remember to bring fun, not just rest. When the Nine does bodywork and awakens to their own body, they become highly magnetic and quite attractive to the Three. The Three loves to see how others are drawn to their Nine and grows healthily protective as the Nine asserts their autonomy. Awakened, they can continue the brave walk toward truth together.

Afterglow: It is wonderful to see a Three and a Nine in harmony because they truly can take on the world. They often roll out the luggage and travel the world together with fun and purpose. Whether they start a business together or just enjoy loads of downtime, they often spend much more than the recommended six to ten hours a week enjoying one another's company. Because there's so much talent and strength in the Three and Nine pairing, others are happy to have them as friends and community leaders. Their scope of influence is both deep and wide.

Type Four with a Type Four

Shine: A Four with another Four in marriage offers a foundational partnership of depth and ideals. They have a shared love for quality time together as well as a desire for profound influence in their corner of the world. Two idealistic Fours offer the whimsical hope that their partner will be exactly as imagined. In early moments of the relationship, this is what happens. With work and dedication toward meaningful exchanges across time, even when ideals aren't met, this couple can extend their early love's gains far into the future.

Heal: One Four can help another to see their worth by being a great listener and empathizing with them about their feelings and experiences. This is rare because a lot of other people are aggressive and assertive or thinking-inhibited and therefore can't or won't give the time of day to these reflections. Since Fours are always trying to figure out who they are, together they allow one another a patient mirror in which to gaze at hope.

Shadows and Throwing Shade: Because both partners are idealists, sometimes their ideals don't line up. Therefore, they disagree about major issues in the world, and if one or both of them are passionate about an issue, it can make for a disconnect. Since they're both withdrawing types, they can ice one another out or try to find someone else to meet their ideals. It's important for them to breathe deeply while remembering that with disparity come interesting conversations, avenues for culture and learning, and more passion together. It's so important that two Fours understand that they must do their bodywork and get proper rest or they won't be able to discharge a lot of the envy and melancholy that they both deal with.

Immerse: Staying in feelings all day can make Fours imbalanced and victimized in their thinking, especially if they're missing out on soul care. They need to remember that God loves them, perfectly imperfect as they are, and that feelings will pass even if it doesn't seem like it. They also need to discharge shame, remembering that everyone needs to have regular therapy or to work on addictions. Finding a satisfying artistic outlet is an extremely important aspect of care, as is a musical outlet or bodywork. These practices can be done mutually or apart, but the work of deciding to be empowered, active, organized, and helpful must be done by both parties across time.

Glow 2.0: When Fours are activated in their minds, bodies, and hearts, they are quite breathtaking to behold, especially if they also have a walk of faith that allows them to see purposes beyond themselves as a couple pairing. People are mesmerized by the way they artfully share what they've created, so boundaries are very important because others will want to spend a lot of time with one or both Fours. Thankfully, Fours enjoy a quiet time of reflecting and relaxing together on their own and will delight in just knowing that they were thought of in many cases. They will also enjoy a few special outings a month with friends and family who adore them.

Afterglow: Fours do well when they get to go outside or to beautiful spaces. They enjoy whimsical experiences from their childhood, and they appreciate these about each other's favorite memories or sites too. They deeply enjoy a trek through a photo book, exploring as they connect. A balance of quality time in and out of the home, together and individually, is of the essence.

Type Four with a Type Five

Shine: A Four and a Five come together in a beautiful iteration of thoughtfulness, creativity, and unusually gifted insight and artistry. They can validate one another's gifts and also access one another's heart and mind, emerging with projects and processes that their own withdrawing and self-doubt would not allow for individually.

Heal: A Four gives a Five stamina and assurance, as the Four wisely sees the value of the Five's beautiful contributions and their potential. The Four enjoys hearing about the research that the Five does, if only for the sake of sheer time together and for the love of having someone so wise. This has the joint benefit of forwarding and developing their own mind even as it makes them feel close to the Five. The Five helps the Four to be brave and to step into action because they believe in the beautiful depths that the Four has discovered about the world. They too are mesmerized by their partner, and both are validated for their often unusual gifts together.

Shadows and Throwing Shade: This pairing can collectively get exhausted from the big seasons of life with work or parenting, so they may retreat for a long while. It is hard for them to decide who will take shifts and get activated when their energy is low and their moods are out of order, and the Four will often wonder why the Five does not reach out to them more to process emotions after some initial withdrawing. They want time together, but they also

231

want space to work on their individual projects. Yet they also have a lot of practical chores to dole out. It's very helpful for this pairing to work off of schedules and share loads. A moral compass also helps them to do the right thing just because it's the right thing, not because they feel like doing it, and thus the Four and Five can begin to understand one another's styles of emotional processing in particular. Music or listening to a podcast can help them to walk through low-energy days with a little more delight.

Immerse: As they emerge in the work of relationships, Fours and Fives realize that they need more than just grit and good planning in order to execute healthy family systems. Spiritual and emotional work also is very important for this sometimes-melancholy duo as they tentatively try to discuss and lean into emotional work together. Working on their deeper issues will take time and resources but will be life-giving. They will come out of their cocoon of stress with strategies for making sure they get enough time for their dates, for their conversations away from kids or other distractions, and for self-care. They will also realize that they each need to continue to have a little bit of independence so they can take turns doing their creative work.

Glow 2.0: It's important for this pairing to set aside strategic time just for the two of them to play and create. They both find so much joy and comfort in their introverted natures together as well as individually. They must attend to their daily fitness routines throughout their lives and continue to advocate for their love in seasons of darkness, often pushing past despair to find the light together. When they're in touch with their feeling, thinking, and doing, as well as their spirituality, they can find that whatever they produce artistically and even systematically helps to raise them out of this despair. The product is a beautiful gift to the world and to their life and legacy together.

Afterglow: Fours and Fives are very helpful to others who are looking to learn from them about the depths of the mind and the heart. They often are part of art, science, faith, or other creative communities and are able to deal with complex cultural issues in healthy ways. They can be peacemakers as well as simply good listeners, helping community members to process trauma with heart and enough keen objectivity and distance to come back to one another and themselves afterward.

Type Four with a Type Six

Shine: At the baseline of the Four and Six bond, there is mutual desire for lots of quality time together and an enamoring with one another's gifts. With the artistry of a Four and the vast attentions and loyalty of the Six, as well as their depths, passion, and thoughtfulness together, this is a caring and compassionate combination.

Heal: The Six very much validates the worth of the Four, not only because of the Four's winsome traits but because they love to have somebody they can be both challenged and enchanted by. Because the Six realizes that relationships are more important than conformity to a large group, they help the Four not to bother ranking themselves against others. Likewise, the Four heals the Six because they don't focus on the mind all the time and can bring the Six into their heart space easily. This is a very welcome and cathartic experience for the Six as they release a lot of stress in the compassionate gaze of the Four.

Shadows and Throwing Shade: The Six can become very jealous of the way that people tend to fawn over the Four or even favor them. The Four, too, can move into their vice of envy since the Six is often quite endearing, funny, attractive, and charming to others.

Because they're both in the Reactive Group, their intensity can rival one another's, and they will occasionally need a third party to help them sort out the major emotions that fly between them, for better or worse.

Immerse: As they work on the relationship, a Six and a Four do well to understand that in addition to their mutual reactivity, they also must process conflict with logic and positivity. The stories that they tell about their relationship must have a positive dynamic thread so they don't stop trusting one another just because of one or two small things that build up over time. They need to be able to discharge angst through bodywork and, if they're spiritual, through prayer, until they've forgiven.

Glow 2.0: When they are both activated in the body center, the Four and Six together are less likely to withdraw in sloth or to withdraw after a heated battle. Instead, they can use their extra positive energy from fitness to have fun and to have deep, healthy dialogue many times and across many years' worth of topics. It's important for this pairing to know that they don't have to feel the same about everything in order to love well. Faith helps here too, as they release ideals and fears to God and not just each other.

Afterglow: Across time, the Six and Four relationship serves the world with their artistry and healthy thinking. They can help one another in their mutual projects and even combine to produce scientific or artistic expression beautifully. As their reactive temperaments feel so deeply, it's important for them to have some time to think on their own, but not for too long. A thirty-minute break to do this helps, as does carving out date nights and weekend adventures just for the two of them for at least six to ten hours a week. No matter how busy they get, this pair loves to connect together.

Type Four with a Type Seven

Shine: The Four and the Seven center their love together through joyfully and authentically listening to one another's hearts, worries, dreams, and hopes. There is a potential for endless conversation and chemistry between these two types, who truly long to help one another experience both the depths of the heart and the joys of the body and head.

Heal: When the Four gives the Seven permission to use their voice authentically and loves them for who they are, imperfections and all, the Seven finds deep comfort. The Seven can slow down and embrace their deeper purposes as they delight in and are mesmerized by the ways the Four takes their time and seems to send a warm glow of love into the world. The Four adores the way the Seven gets them moving, makes them laugh, and encourages them to turn their dreams into reality.

Shadows and Throwing Shade: Even though both the Four and the Seven are idealists, sometimes their ideals are differing or even in contrast, such as in the way the Four slows down when anxious and the Seven speeds up. At times, the Four needs to take time to think slowly and just be by themselves, but sometimes the Seven can be judgmental and think the Four is withholding love just to be cruel. What they have to understand is that the Four is dealing with a deep envy for the way the Seven seems to move through life so quickly, and they are both just overwhelmed by the pace.

Immerse: As they immerse in feelings work, especially if there's a big lapse of trust, it's helpful for this couple to work together but also individually. The Seven must learn to release feelings instead of just criticizing, and the Four must learn to engage in confidence, not withdraw in despair. They may need professionals to walk them through this journey.

Glow 2.0: The Four and Seven together bring honesty, depth, love, light, and fun. Because of their magnetism, they meet interesting people in the world. Even when alone, they draw upon mental and artistic reflections so they can reach one another's hearts and ultimately their family and community with wisdom, joy, and genuine love.

Afterglow: This beautiful pairing loves time just to indulge in their bond. They will always be very refreshed by intentional date nights. When a Four and Seven are teaming up on projects, they do well to find an ideal they both share and to then craft separate pieces. This brings the couple together as they reach their community with depth of feeling and beauty as well as hope, joy, and healthy mental gifts. If the Four is able to come into presence and the Seven is able to focus, their beautiful adventure is felt vibrantly around the world together.

Type Four with a Type Eight

Shine: A Four and an Eight draw their love from a passionate, vibrant, and captivating space together, creating a bond that is full of both tender pauses and powerful momentum. The Four appreciates the practical leadership gifts of the Eight, who shines in the world with justice, strength, and power, while the Eight appreciates the mesmerizing beauty, compassion, and idealistic but fiery hopes of the Four.

Heal: Across time, the Four gives the typically invulnerable Eight a safe place to process the more sensitive feelings they have shut off to the hard world. The polarity of this experience offers them both a layer of healing. Thus, finding love in one another's unconditional support is an almost insatiable need for both parties as they continually seek out these affirmations of their belovedness.

Shadows and Throwing Shade: Because the Four is a withdrawing type who needs time to process their overwhelming feelings and the Eight moves so quickly and stoically in their aggressive nature, over time the styles that were once enchanting to each of them can rub up against them. For instance, when the Eight doesn't always respect the space that the Four needs, the Eight retaliates instead of just honoring the brief time needed to process. The Eight, feeling wounded, can be cold or vengeful, regretful that they leaned in to love and sorrowful that they have put their big heart out on the line.

Immerse: The Eight and the Four each need bodywork in order to work off their steam, and the Eight will likely need a more intense workout than the Four, who can find fulfillment in soulful meditation, a solo jog, dance, or worship movements. The Eight also has to respect that the Four has their own voice, thoughts, and ideas that may differ from their own decisive angle, and the Four may likewise shudder at differing ideals. It may take a mentor they both respect to affirm for them that it is not a weakness but an actual strength to find a bond across differences. The Four must likewise discharge envy of other individuals or couples, replacing it with gratitude.

Glow 2.0: As they stabilize their polarity, this pairing has the potential for great heights. The Eight is thrilled to have a partner with a passion that matches their own, especially since the Four has the gifts of both presence and pausing, which are helpful to the Eight's constant forward thrust that is part of their very soul. The Four is equally willing to make sure that the Eight feels seen and celebrated in their big accomplishments and ultimately loves how the Eight drives them forward out of self-doubt and into the rush of life.

Afterglow: Since life is often long and since many people find them each so captivating, this couple needs to continually nurture one another's hearts with scheduling in fun and romance amid their passion projects. They can also intentionally partake of the simple, everyday miracles of love together as they combine their pacing with the balance this now seasoned pair can craft so well. Amid their grand plans to change the world together, they also do well to take ample time just for the two of them and with their family in tranquil and aesthetically appealing corners of the world.

Type Four with a Type Nine

Shine: A Four and a Nine love playful and romantic retreats alike, as well as engaging with the world in caring, passionate, and fun-filled ways. Though they may not share all of life's rhythms on a daily basis, they find in one another an enthusiasm for sharing the depths of their souls and dreams. The Four validates and values the gifts of the Nine because they see all that the Nine has to offer in the world, gifts they themselves are even envious about at times. The Nine doesn't want the Four to feel jealous and works hard to make them feel special, unique, and important. In this way, they help one another to rise up out of their withdrawing stances.

Heal: The Nine helps the Four to realize they have intrinsic value, something the Four greatly struggles with. The Nine also helps the Four to stay within their body more and to have fun doing relaxing things after long, hard days. Across time, the Nine is quite patient with the Four and can be a great listener and advice giver, which helps the Four to gain confidence in the world. Meanwhile, the Four loves to be near the peaceful heart of a Nine, deeply drinking in the Nine's calm and present countenance.

Shadows and Throwing Shade: When the Nine doesn't want to discuss issues, the Four may not understand their boundaries and may think that the Nine never wants to discuss anything. This may even be true. Also, the Four can be very codependent at times and lean on the Nine much too hard for their self-efficacy, burdening the

Nine with their dependency. The Nine would rather have comfort in relaxation and not always have to hold the Four up, especially since the Four already typically has a captivated audience of their own in the world. The Nine's anger over all the ways they aren't heard is not hidden from the Four, and they may both withdraw for too long. This mutual withdrawing is difficult for the marriage because someone has to lean in and pursue.

Immerse: Doing their immersion work for the Four and the Nine means exactly that: work. Action is so important. When they put healthy communication and conflict-addressing tips into place and each find their own comfortable and safe routes to healing, this pairing is a classic and mesmerizing model of love and fun to their peers. Because both of these types are doing-inhibited, bodywork and spiritual releasing are essential. Incorporating massage, fitness, or other body routines does a world of difference to wake them up to joy and to the life and passion within.

Glow 2.0: As the Nine opens up and confidence begins to develop as they do their bodywork, the Four will see their extra energy and find their strength and newfound awareness admirable. The Four will find validation for their belovedness from their wide-awake, loving Nine, resulting in a glorious glow. But even as the Nine embraces more healthy emotions, the Four will need to set some comfortable bounds around reactive tendencies so together they can more consistently shine out in the world with a brighter light.

Afterglow: This couple does well to find a system each year for a schedule and routine that allows the Four some creativity and flexibility but does not overextend their slower pace or take advantage of the good-hearted, robust, vigorous Nine. They can do this by talking out their visions for the weeks, months, and years they are in and by encouraging but not pushing each other into their endeavors. Planning and scheduling allows this pairing to use their gifts of justice fighting, artistry, and compassion in the world as they enchant others with their winsome, easy, and mutually attentive model bond.

Type Five with a Type Five

Shine: The playful and fascinating dance of two Fives is one of mutual understanding and privacy, passionate love, and intelligence. In both their obsession with research and their resistance to overdoing, two Fives carry themselves with wisdom, patience, and wit. They are both able to withdraw from the world when they need rest, and they generally respect this about the other as well.

Heal: Many people in the life of a Five do not understand the measured energy that they have for each day. Another Five does understand this, however, and the need for privacy is not perceived as a lack of love but as a replenishing of resources and anxiety management. This shared struggle against the vice of avarice is understood by both in times of perceived scarcity. Being respected versus rejected by one another gives them gentle encouragement to step into the world a little more boldly and to share their many gifts after their rest is over.

Shadows and Throwing Shade: As with any withdrawing pairing, this couple has a tendency to not discuss issues. Though some of the issues will naturally take care of themselves in the mind of the practical Five, others do need to be addressed and will unfortunately fester without attention. Fives are also at risk for not spending energy and time on each other because of their fascinating individual pursuits—pursuits they may even be compartmentalizing with others. Fives can rationalize unhealthy coping styles to protect themselves and dissipate anxiety, and as they can feel a lack of guilt over such mental escapades, they may at times cross poor boundaries with money, addiction, or another person.

Immerse: Doing their mutual work for this pairing means indulging their minds, taking care of their bodies on a regular basis, and doing heart-to-heart check-ins with each other, even if they're using the language of thoughts. A check-in could be as simple as briefly sharing the highs and lows of the day, but they should also make plans to immerse themselves in the five senses so they can deepen their heart connection. They may love movies or music as a release, or perhaps there is a spiritual component of release for them. A pair of Fives must work on self-efficacy as well so they don't look for their spouse or others to confirm or reject their worth; they have worth as they are.

Glow 2.0: Fives who are activated with head, body, and heart balance know how to speak to one another's hearts through that language. They know how to compromise and save energy for each other, and slowly but surely, they can be coaxed to assert themselves in the world, both together and apart, with their wonderful wisdom.

Afterglow: Two Fives show up with playfulness, wit, fun, adventure, creativity, and a whole lot of love. Their relationship is quieter than a lot of other couples, but their love is just as deep, if not deeper, as they prefer one another over others. Fives can also stop and bask in their past and current contributions, realizing that there will always be ongoing research in the world and that they don't have to do it all. They can enjoy freedom, wonder, and a sense of synergistic flow, because they know that their energy comes from rest and research but also shared activity at times.

Type Five with a Type Six

Shine: Both the depths of conversation and the light, playful banter of the Five and Six are a staple feature of their relationship. They never tire of coming back for more wit and banter as they playfully tease and flirt with one another, both deeply loving but also deeply aware of the vulnerability of a heart connection. This practical pair is a savvy duo, and they love thinking up creative ways to multiply their resources with their tactical brainpower. They also enjoy basking in the comfort of each other after long, hard days.

Heal: A Five loves to take care of the vulnerabilities of the Six and to protect their needs practically and efficiently. They rightly take pride in doing this for their Six, who is often looking for some leadership features and a partner. The Six loves to nurture the Five and patiently tries to understand the Five on a deeper mental level than anyone else has ever been allowed to. Their patience with one another allows for healing experiences together and a thoughtful, healthy, slow-burning but long-lasting glow.

Shadows and Throwing Shade: As much as these two fast-thinking types love to dialogue and debate their plans for shaping the world, when they get into the pursuer-distancer cycle of a relationship, it's hard for one or the other to step out of their very natural roles of pursuer (Six) and distancer (Five). However, as in most relationships, some interplay and polarity is needed, especially with these mentally rich types. Without their playful side, the Six can be very overwhelming to the Five in their relentless pursuit for connection. Likewise, the Five can feel very cold and distant to the Six, and they can both spiral down in worry and overwhelm.

Immerse: Finding a practical marriage helper or trusted mentor is often a key part to the success of the Five and Six so they can address things with order, wisdom, a sense of humor, and a realistic

242

time frame, and so they can get a break from one another's over-analysis. It's healthy for them to have somebody they can come to season by season when difficulties come up. On their own and/ or with a helper, they will both do well to create positive stories about their partner when their minds threaten to take them into dark spaces, and they will be challenged to continue to maintain positivity and fun as well.

Glow 2.0: It's wonderful to see a Five and a Six who have planned not just for their vast learning in the world but also for their love and romance to blossom. The world is very touched when they see the fierce, quiet, and deep sensual love of this passionate pair as they emanate wisdom, fun, and playful love together in the world.

Afterglow: A Five and a Six will always go back to feeling like they don't have enough personal resources, but depriving each other of their most treasured self-soothing resources will not work for a healthy relationship. Sometimes their self-soothing habits will need to be changed for various reasons, so flexibility is of the essence, even though both types love to plan. The Five may not share things that they think the Six will be afraid of, so part of their afterglow together is making sure that they openly address issues and healthy strategies on a weekly basis over coffee, during a walk, or in a planner that they do together. This helps them be on the same page and also have some healthy freedoms of planning their own lives.

Type Five with a Type Seven

Shine: A Five and a Seven make for a deep, safe, and soulful connection. Though they share a wry perspective on the world's ability to understand and be able to give to them, as a pair, they are deeply connected and finally have a safe harbor. Their creative mental wheels are constantly working in tandem to influence the world in organized, efficient, and fun problem-solving ways.

Heal: There is an unspoken agreement between thinking types since both realize that safety is an essential quality to survival. The Five helps the Seven to savor life and enter into deeper realms of discovery and focus, and the Seven helps the Five to step into their body center and enjoy life more optimistically. They often have high verbal acuity for practical problem-solving as they jointly dream dreams and find ways to interestingly, efficiently, and ethically help the world.

Shadows and Throwing Shade: A Five and a Seven can both be reactive when their plans are challenged, yet they have opposing ways of responding. When the Seven gets emotional or defensive, they reach out in hot pursuit of connecting and finding a compromise. This is overwhelming to the Five, who withdraws in the face of wild emotion and quick solutions that may seem like an unnecessary risk when they could play it safer. Because it feels threatening to the Five to deal with somebody who is out of control or overwhelming, and it feels threatening to the Seven to be ignored when they have finally admitted need, the couple's pursuer-distancer dance can lead to a cycle of neither intimacy nor problems getting solved.

Immerse: A Five and a Seven must learn to balance their overactive minds, not just with logical thoughts but with body and heart work. This means vulnerability, which is hard for both types. When they feel safe to open their hearts—which will require some logical and thoughtful processing together or possibly the assistance of a skilled third party such as a Gottman or an EFT therapist—they are much more likely to communicate in healthy ways rather than reactively or dismissively. They also need some faith, which can also be difficult for both types, who tend to be somewhat skeptical of authority. They need to fight the fear that comes from letting go of the reins and trust the process to work.

Glow 2.0: When Fives and Sevens have learned to compromise and find vulnerability, even admitting weakness together, there are few avenues of love that go untapped, since each is more eager than the other to prove their love to one another. Others can't help but admire their deeply romantic vibe as they give space and liftoff for one another's dreams to be pursued and at times to intertwine.

Afterglow: Because of the active minds of this dynamic duo, they do well to take regularly scheduled dates doing something adventurous or fun or academically interesting together. They can take time in the body center as well as celebrate in bigger ways. They love planning quality time together that allows them to sit in the wonder of creation and remember nature's greatest gifts to them, including each other. Because of their gratitude for these natural wonders and their shared love and wisdom, they have an eminence of joy and wisdom to pass to a broken world.

Type Five with a Type Eight

Shine: The focus and self-control of the Five and the vibrant and far-reaching energy of an Eight provide an irresistible synergy of wisdom, strength, and productivity. Together they can reach deeply into ideas and execute them with energy and focus that is rarely seen. They plunge the depths of life and emerge with inspiration and wisdom for achieving their goals. After their vast explorations across their uncharted life and marriage path, they love retreating into rest as needed.

Heal: An Eight initially heals the insecurity and competency issues in a Five by encouraging them and keeping them moving and on mission. They also don't mind carrying out some of the more energetic tasks of the family system as long as the Five finds ways to help and defend the Eight. A Five naturally heals an Eight by encouraging them to slow down and to dive deeper in order to achieve their big goals with success and focused stamina.

Shadows and Throwing Shade: When a Five and an Eight cannot temper their opposing desires to control, they may face volatility, especially since both deal with rejection and anger. Another negative move they can make is a natural and stubborn withdrawal. Along with this stalemate, a Five or an Eight may feel apathy or anger about being the one to make the first move back toward the other. Another possible shadow for this couple is in their verbal diatribes, which are hard to forget even for these strong but sensitive types.

Immerse: Immersing in the work of this pairing requires that the Five step into life with courage and synergy. The Eight also must realize that their partner's goals, not just theirs, are important and that compromise, mutual respect, and some space are needed. Their earlier belief that their way is the one right way and that other perspectives don't have validity will not suffice. The same can be said of the Five, who often gets locked in one mindset. As both types lean in, even if they choose to agree to disagree on some fronts, they must be willing to understand and implement forgiveness practices as well as to agree to times of retreat and autonomy.

Glow 2.0: There is excitement in merging in the world of activity and rest. There, the Five and Eight engage with their newfound knowledge and life-giving advice and strength. Once this pairing comes to realize that all perspectives have value and that compromise will (shockingly) not kill them, there's an excitement and healthy immersion into the world of synergy as they swim through the seas of love with strength in tandem.

Afterglow: Both the Five and the Eight are very relational, and they love serving those truly less fortunate. The Five will help the Eight to tap into resources of rest, while the Eight will challenge the Five to build endurance and healthy resistance to outward stress so there is a longer tolerance of unpleasant stimuli. With this unique interchange of gifts, they exercise their emotional, physical, and mental muscles and share their findings with the world.

Type Five with a Type Nine

Shine: The Five and the Nine bond over their desire to hold space for one another and to be fully safe and rested together. They derive safety and comfort from one another's unexpectant presence and are thereby an oasis of love and coziness. Their bond is often felt internally more than externally in their mutual desire to not overdo but to explore without hurry across time. In response to a very active world that will irritate and pull at them, the Five and the Nine love that their partner does not have ideas about life that feel too grandiose. They appreciate the practicality, sacrifice, logic, and commitment to hard work that each brings to the marriage.

Heal: Often the Five is very observant and will see the wonderful ways that a Nine contributes to the world, which many others miss out on. They remind the Nine not to run too fast to please others and will help them to set boundaries so others don't take advantage of them. The Nine appreciates the Five's wisdom, especially in areas they are not skilled in, and that may create convenience, efficiency, and comfort for the Nine. This can carry forward if the Five continues to be thoughtful instead of doing what most people do to a Nine, which is take advantage of their agreeableness over time. The Nine also understands the limited energy of the Five and allows the Five to heal in introverted rest.

Shadows and Throwing Shade: If the Five takes advantage of the kindness of the Nine and lets them do everything, the Nine will grow deeply resentful of the load they carry for the family and act out overtly or, more often, passive-aggressively. Instead of building a hierarchy in a relationship, the Nine demands democracy, and their kindness will not be mistaken for weakness. However, as a five-senses body type, they may also wax critical on their Five, enacting the rejection of the Five, who will concede to all the Nine's critiques of them.

Immerse: A Five and a Nine must take precious energy and resources to work on relationship conflict actively so they are getting regular accountability and not just shoving their conflicts under a rug with no solutions. They also must acknowledge that both parties have strengths and areas for growth. Not playing tit-for-tat is key, since each season of marriage will require different energy from each type. Negative storytelling by the Nine must be replaced with assertiveness for their needs and a reminder of the positive aspects of their Five, especially since the Five is reticent to speak up for their positive attributes at times. This pair does well to get daily active body care in, especially surrounding fitness, as well as to take getaways once or twice a year to remember the fun they share together, not just independently.

Glow 2.0: As they start awakening together, the Five and Nine must plan for six to ten hours a week for regular date nights so they can keep the romance flowing, even if it doesn't look or feel like a traditional romance. As best friends, they will find plenty to do, and they don't need the approval of the world to do it, letting the "shoulds" of others fall off. Their quiet and unassuming bond is fierce, and the lengths and heights they go to in order to protect one another in action speak much louder than words.

Afterglow: This pairing does not want a lot of accolades for doing what they believe is right and good in the world—at least not publicly—which may make them feel them bound to a type of giving that feels too taxing when they are already sensitive to fatigue. Ongoing bodywork will keep them more energized as they find release from their planning processes and connect more within their bodies. When healthy, this pair offers generous and fun gifts to one another and the community. They keep their bond with safety, logic, and some lightness, maintaining good boundaries for the long haul.

Type Six with a Type Six

Shine: Two Sixes in marriage come together with natural intelligence, a knack for planning, and a love for comfortability and style. In their bond, each Six discovers that they've found a partner who can troubleshoot and pause as needed to plan for safety in the relationship with good balance and boundaries. It's helpful for a Six to have a partner who understands the need to pivot when new plans and ideas are thrust into the day. They bring humor, wit, a love of rest, and a deep love of family.

Heal: Sixes have a unique ability to heal one another because they have finally found a partner who understands the importance of planning and preparing. They each help their spouse to plan well, they enjoy listening to their spouse's ideas, and they give them strategies and tips for healing, actively troubleshooting, and helping one another avoid missteps and disasters. After the planning is done, they love to relax and just enjoy reflection and peace together.

Shadows and Throwing Shade: Because Sixes can project any number of negative stories onto their partner and the world in a matter of seconds, they can go down together in a depressive spiral, overanalyzing quickly and becoming frozen in dread, tuning out to television or other indirect coping strategies. It is important that they learn self-soothing techniques as they immerse themselves in the work of positivity and logic, not just reactivity. Otherwise, they will end up being paranoid and sickly and causing one another worsening anxiety.

Immerse: Because of their propensity to massively overanalyze with their vast intelligence, it's important that two Sixes take a team approach as they get healthy. This includes taking outside advice since they can get lost in their own heads. They benefit from hiring a coach or counselor who won't do the work for them but who will help them to sort it all out. In that work, Sixes will face compromises, a need for higher spiritual work and letting go, and redemption as they forgive one another for past mistakes, slowly but surely.

Glow 2.0: As they move away from anxiety and slothful checking out, it's helpful for Sixes to remember that two to three and a half hours a day is the recommended time for rest for most people to have a happy life. They should continue to care for their physical and mental health on an ongoing basis. They may even need to take certain dietary measures, such as cutting out caffeine or adding in a cardio workout, as they realize that having too much energy contributes to their anxiety.

Afterglow: Since there's always more work to do, Sixes together do well to stick to their routines and lists so their minds don't stray from their priorities, including being grounded enough to think of one another. Sixes are also prone to thinking about stressful topics and being negative, so it's important that they help one another watch out for that and plan just-for-fun excursions regularly. It's a beautiful thing to see Sixes in their fun and restfulness after they've made courageous moves. They really love to relax together!

Type Six with a Type Seven

Shine: A Six and a Seven attract one another as kindred spirits as they mutually move in their environment with mental agility, wit, and intelligence. Together they rise up with verbal acuity and a quickness of mind that is unrivaled. Since each is able to articulate and to verbally spar ideas, they find conversation with one another fascinating as they collectively reach new depths of safety and understanding.

Heal: The Six feels protected by the savvy and energized Seven, who has a positive plan for everything, is able to troubleshoot the fears of the Six, and does not admit defeat. The Six in turn offers heartfelt care to the world-weary Seven. The Six is also a safe place for the Seven to share their real feelings and concerns. The Seven may have felt like they were pulling the weight of the world before they met the Six, but now they feel true partnership. The Six is able and willing to help them execute plans with order, fluidity, and style—details the Seven can miss in their quest to run fast and hard in their planning.

Shadows and Throwing Shade: The Seven feels baited by the reactivity and emotionality of the Six. In fact, they can downright reject the Six if they are already afraid of being overwhelmed or too busy. When the Six retreats in hurt, the Seven often runs away emotionally, if not physically. They feel unable to stop long enough to consider that they aren't supportive to their loyal Six in their concerns because of their own dark fears, and instead they become critical. The Seven likes to stay happy and optimistic, fully knowing the Six takes them down a path to realism or even an existential despair that they are afraid they will not emerge from. It's imperative that this couple doesn't just gloss over issues, even those that seem insurmountably daunting.

Immerse: It's of utmost importance for the Six and Seven to work together on building safety for sharing emotional intimacy together. Preferably with a professional or mentor, the pair can work on processing the hefty emotions from the Six as well as the hidden concerns of the Seven. The Six must learn to be compassionate and resist hysteria about the fact that the seemingly invulnerable Seven is afraid of dark feelings. The Six must expect to find several outlets for their anxiety, even when the Seven does learn tolerance, and this especially includes doing bodywork. Since the Six must also respect the Seven's coping style of physicality, they may even find some of this release of excess anxiety together.

Glow 2.0: As the Six and Seven learn to open up their mind, body, and hearts more expansively and find limitations from their spouse, they also must realize God can help them in areas their spouse cannot. They love each other with less forceful, controlling behaviors and allow small, gentle reinforcements for the strides they see in one another across time. It also helps when this couple realizes that not everybody is a thinking type like them. As they incorporate community support, it's best that they set boundaries around emotional topics and work to become one another's safe place.

Afterglow: It's wonderful for a Six and a Seven to openly and vulnerably discuss feelings and problems together as they troubleshoot. But it's even sweeter to see them work hard and then take time to rest and relax to enjoy one another's company. Because they have the potential to be excellent thought leaders in the world, both need mental rest to make it for the long haul. Whether they're taking mentally releasing walks or blaring music on drives together, it's important that they find special times of eating, relaxing, and being physical so they take ownership of the fact that they want to bring balance in their marriage, not just in separate communities.

Type Six with a Type Eight

Shine: A Six and an Eight find in one another strong allies as they both love with passion and fight together for justice. They combine with mental and physical strength and in shared passion over their common goals of safety, justice, and empowerment in the world. They find their stride in working in tandem as well. The Six brings the Eight to a slower pace and to a more careful nurturing of relationships and planning. The Eight brings the Six the thrill of stepping into life with power, and together their gifts pave the way for completing their dreams.

Heal: The Eight finds safety and a willingness to be vulnerable with their extremely loyal Six, as well as an alignment of values with their sharp, witty, and thoughtful comrade. The Six finds the longed-for security in the protective, relational stance of the Eight, who also helps them to address their scattered or fearful thoughts and step into their virtue of courage.

Shadows and Throwing Shade: The Six can become overwhelmed by the extremely rapid pace of an Eight, especially if the Eight does not slow down long enough to heed the troubleshooting caution of the Six, who must have sanctions in place to feel able to move forward. On the contrary, the Eight may feel the Six is weak or cowardly and express disgust for them, and the Six may recoil in fear and hurt. Either one may reach out to a third party for emotional support at this stalemate or retaliate in other ways.

Immerse: It's very important that both the Six and the Eight incorporate head, body, and heart healing in order to balance their extreme positioning as two reactive types. An ongoing spiritual component is also essential for both parties to truly forgive and build back trust over time. They need respect for both their own and their partner's divergent gifts, which, when used in tandem, can help them glow much brighter. As they immerse, they do well to make space for one another's approaches as well as to pause and take deep breaths as needed. Having a third-party helper is a good idea from time to time.

Glow 2.0: For ongoing balance, the Six and Eight can hold their ground together in their abilities to express themselves directly. As they each lean in to communicate, it's beautiful to see them listen to one another's hearts, which helps them learn to have enough faith to compromise. As they begin to see that others' styles of engagement also have wisdom, mutual respect for one another's gifts will grow. Since the Six is a head type and the Eight is a body type, as long as they can both continue to stand strong in their particular gifts, over time they will continue to learn from each other as well as come to know what to expect from each other—a loyalty they both love.

Afterglow: This pair can stay positive by replacing negative stories and suppositions about one another with positivity and logic. They sometimes need a brief time to cool down. When the air is cleared, they love reuniting after their arguments and planning adventures. Doing ongoing bodywork and finding a healthy release of emotions helps as well. With all their reactivity, they get some extremely wonderful highs and some very low lows, so it's okay for them to remind each other that over-the-counter or prescribed medication is an option.

Type Six with a Type Nine

Shine: From the earliest days, the Six and the Nine bond over not only their mutual desire for material comfort and tranquility but also their skilled planning and practicality. They care about one another deeply and greatly need the other's strengths to sharpen them and wake them from their dormant issues. Together, they bring peace and the best of planning with their multiple harmonic traits.

Heal: It's wonderful for the Nine to have a chance to step into their natural leadership qualities when the Six is looking for advice and leadership. Nines can also be great at talking the Six off the ledge with their strong and wise advice as well as their calming perspective. While the Nine doesn't want to make *all* decisions for the Six, it helps them to feel like they have a voice and that their wisdom is valued and appreciated. Together, this pair strategizes and supports well. These features of offering peace and receiving wisdom were not always easily accessed during formative years.

Shadows and Throwing Shade: The Six can be overly reactive while the Nine erroneously believes that they must be in a harmonious, peaceful state at all times. When the couple feels overwhelmed and disharmonious, they often withdraw in hysteria, despair, or mutual sloth and despondency. The Nine can get overwhelmed and triggered by pushing down their anxiety and not facing things. When their anxiety does erupt, they fear potentially triggering the Six's anxiety to even greater levels, causing them to try to bottle up even more. When the Six pursues too heavily, it only hurts the Nine, who needs space and autonomy.

Immerse: It's very important that both the Six and the Nine work on their hidden and overt anxiety or depression issues. Both are sensitive in their body centers, so they need to do their bodywork and eat well as needs arise or even as preventative care, reminding one another of this importance at varying times since they often share the same struggles. When either enters into a position of nonconformity on an important marriage issue—which may show up as apathy and stubbornness for the Nine and paranoia or hyperarousal for the Six—they may need additional third-party support. They are, however, greatly helped by body care, journaling, and walks and talks to get their anxieties moving up and out.

Glow 2.0: As this couple works on their anxiety and does their bodywork, their own clear voices emerge with clarity, and they can begin to trust themselves and their special and mutual gifts more readily. When inner trust develops, they can become safe and confident listeners together, building one another up with more consistency and diplomatically finding the roles where they best serve the family and community. The Nine has a lot of power and strength, and the Six has much wisdom. As they rise up into their bodywork and voicing their needs, they are no longer hiding from the world in a shadowy or sleepy way but shining brightly.

Afterglow: Now that this pair knows how to wake up, how to use their voices, and how to help the afterglow of their love last, they need to have regular check-ins with each other as well as regular date nights to stay active. They need rest together and individually so they can effortlessly and efficiently move in rhythm like very few couples can. They often work alone or in tandem in healthy rhythms, each achieving their goals with the support of one an-other's complementary gifts and glow.

Type Seven with a Type Seven

Shine: Two Sevens find many shared rhythms and interests with their ever-processing minds, their mutual desire for uninhibited creativity, and their appreciation for freedom and fluid motion. They both dream big and work hard, executing their dreams with precision amid the self-soothing indulgences that balance them. As two idealists, they have freedom to pursue their goals, no apologies required.

Heal: It's a gift to have a partner who gets the incessant, inquisitive, kinetic learning of a Seven. Two Sevens understand this as well as almost everything between them that goes unsaid, such as the emotions that often lay dormant. This understanding also allows them to give one another space in focused times of self-care, to take feelings in small doses, and to dote on one another with an intimate mental knowing.

Shadows and Throwing Shade: If one or both Sevens are too scattered, leaving goals unfinished or unmanaged, they can become very critical of each other for being less than perfect. They may collectively get so lost in their passion projects that they delay or ignore aspects of self or family care. Two idealists also don't always share the same ideals. Instead of always running to the next thing, they both have to acknowledge that their gift and virtue is sobriety, allowing their minds to rest daily for long-term mental, physical, and emotional health and presence. They must remember that sheer hedonism finds its end early.

Immerse: Two Sevens may be charming to others as a couple, but even if they have a lot of good problem-solving skills and playful vibes, there are still issues they have to work out. They must learn to lean in to one another's needs, which will create some friction at least momentarily, with one or both feeling less safe as head types. Because Sevens have grown up thinking they can't rely on anyone but themselves, a foundational aspect of walking toward health or recovery for them is building trust. As idealists, they need to acknowledge and regularly lament the fact that nobody is perfect, not even them, and that even though their spouse has disappointed them, forgiveness is of the essence. A Seven needs to give their partner the same grace they give themselves, and when this happens, joy and fun return.

Glow 2.0: When Sevens have learned to respect one another's space, finish projects, dream together, and allow their spouse to critique them with love and grace, the sky is really the limit on what they can accomplish in terms of building creative projects or engineering new systems together. Intentionally building emotional connections and having rest time both together and apart will help them to shine brightly together in a major way.

Afterglow: Two thoughtful Sevens come to realize that slowing down will not kill them but will actually allow for grit and grace. Instead of running, they can set the pace to walking and take short breaks. The limits they set together will also increase trust with others, who learn that this couple can be counted on to not over-book and underdeliver. Building trust also happens inside the marriage as they develop tenacity together. This is a beautiful thing because they can now share all their ideas in the world and even work on projects together with a lot of grace. The ever-refining productions of two Sevens allow for richness and depth, compassion and rest.

Type Seven with a Type Eight

Shine: The Seven and Eight glow is a bright and dynamic pairing. Together they create a dazzling display of love on the move. They find comfort in the mutual understanding of the love of the game and of life. They both also appreciate the worthy undertaking of making one's own mark on the world and know how to have fun, to learn, and to take their dreams seriously with action. There's an absolute guarantee of sparks and fireworks as they light up the darkness with their kinetic energy.

Heal: Eights can help Sevens strategize through their inner fears with power and resistance. Likewise, fast-thinking Sevens can be very helpful in problem-solving for the powerful but sometimes thinking-inhibited Eight. Having the protection of a healthy, solid Eight feels very secure and comforting for a Seven. The strong mind of a Seven helps an Eight get their ideas off the ground, making the Eight exceptionally grateful.

Shadows and Throwing Shade: Although they are vibrant, even the most brilliant lights eventually burn out. When they each lose their steam, the Seven and Eight grow tired and intolerant of one another's formerly merely annoying patterns and often loudly complain. The Seven may run away when the Eight goes too far, and both will need to work on what to do when emotional flooding occurs. They can also do third-party work, whether it be with a mentor or a friend. It will be important for this couple to work on self-control, do bodywork to discharge extra energy, and make sure logic and boundaries are involved, as they can get emotionally reactive quickly.

Immerse: This extremely active pairing must learn how to stay engaged and how to compromise even when their spouse is imperfect. Since both of these types tend to distrust, they can have a hard time forgiving others who have hurt them. It is very important these individuals seek spirituality, as their strong bodies and minds can create a stubborn stronghold. Only tenacity and a determination to grow, paired with intentional grace, will help.

Glow 2.0: This couple emerges from doing their work with power, victory, and pride. They must avoid having an arrogant glow at the finish line as the world watches them win together. Not everyone has their power, but they all have other, equally important gifts. This couple also does well to serve the world, not just each other, as they remember that true life satisfaction comes not only from excess and reward but from helping other people.

Afterglow: No matter the season, it's a gift for others to behold and be near this kinetic-powered pairing. As the Seven and Eight line up, they must respect one another, realizing that together their impact is greater. Both need to remember that no one is perfect and that slowing down to access their heart connection is vital. As they learn the value of self-observation and balancing their hearts along with their active minds and bodies, this pairing begins to more deeply find solace in one another's arms after long, hard days and to prioritize meaningful events with collaboration and compromise.

Type Seven with a Type Nine

Shine: The Seven and Nine pair find one another with their shared love for the good, the true, and the beautiful. They love to make one another feel seen and special. They easily champion one another's many gifts, which others often overlook with judgment or misunderstanding. A Nine and a Seven together balance both energy and rest. In their natural bond, they can grow and explore without worrying that the other will try to overtake their freedom, and they can find safety in each other's positive and strong love time and again.

Heal: The Nine offers the Seven a space to rest in play and to talk. In turn, the Seven offers the Nine encouragement and awakens them to the limitless possibilities in their lives. The Nine also soothes the Seven's deep anxiety and offers them a supportive structure from which to move and rest.

Shadows and Throwing Shade: A Seven can push too hard on a Nine and overwhelm them, fearing the Nine will run away in anger and complacence. The Seven can quickly read the stubbornness of the Nine and will push harder on them. When this happens, the Nine often resists and goes within themselves. The Seven will also give up on or resist the Nine if the Nine feels boring or sedate. Instead of bringing one another to life and balance, they can overemphasize positivity and pleasures. This can make them not face their problems and leave them with major differences that never get discussed.

Immerse: Since neither type easily shares vulnerable feelings, it's very important that they get third-party support as needed to process together and individually. A huge part of their success involves making a daily list—created together and fairly divided—and sticking to it, then rewarding themselves when the list has been achieved. The Seven has to learn self-soothing so they don't lean too hard on the Nine for all their comfort. The Nine needs to release anger via physical fitness and find their own empowerment through bodywork.

Glow 2.0: This couple does well to regularly be vulnerable and open up their feelings to one another, not just to indulge in pleasure. They must stay open long enough to let one another and other people in, even though it's not always natural. They also need to set up a specified time that is just for them to replenish together.

Afterglow: Because the Nine helps the Seven to enjoy their introverted side a bit more, they can both work on beautiful, focused projects individually as well as a couple and learn to relax together across time. Their collective outpouring shows their depths and successes in a variety of fields. It's lovely to see the way they can bring their peaceful yet bright glow out to the world with their bursts of advocacy, wisdom, peace, and joy.

Type Eight with a Type Eight

Shine: Two Eights find in one another a strength and an energy to meet their goals and desires with passion. They encourage one another with direct communication, robust energy, practicality, and the ability to champion and celebrate a job well done. This pairing often cares about helping the underserved together as well.

Heal: Because Eights usually find resistance in the community in terms of how much energy they put into their projects and interests, it's wonderful to have someone who understands their drive and often tireless passion. They both offer a partnership of understanding, accepting the realization that vulnerability is hard and scary. Together, they create a warm glow of love across time as they nurture and respect one another's strengths and offer softness and advocacy.

Shadows and Throwing Shade: Because Eights have such a large passion for life, sometimes their ideals and goals will not match up. They will resent one another at times for their competing large visions. Since both often vie for the position of leader with such a large passion for life, they lead with aggression, which does not lead to intimacy and is then followed by complete withdrawal by both parties.

Immerse: Eights need to take turns addressing hurts directly, taking pauses and deep breaths to decrease frequent emotional flooding. Even with their disparity, they then choose forgiveness and trusting God's justice so they can release vengeance. With strong personality dynamics, they need someone wise and energized to help them strategize. Both Eights must find ways for their large appetites to have interesting work and space to play, as well as to form safe neutral space together for recovery from the day. They each need a bodily release of stress at least once daily, as well as some space for privacy. Reading, researching, studying, or just having quiet time is helpful for an hour or so a day.

Glow 2.0: Once the Eights have both learned to take rest and get bodily release, they need ongoing weekly meetings to talk about how to plan, balance, and integrate opinions and core values together, as well as how to advocate and support one another in those goals. They can then use the rest of their massive energy to work hard on their goals and to celebrate one another and themselves well.

Afterglow: After serving with their energy and huge hearts in the world and encountering their daily tasks, Eights together can experience rest and relaxation to the best of their abilities. They both understand that their love can be a vulnerable yet strong private oasis to balance out all they're giving publicly. They can celebrate and champion one another like no other.

Type Eight with a Type Nine

Shine: An Eight and a Nine in marriage come together in safety and strength, validating one another's voice and powerful presence. The strength of the Eight paves the way for the Nine to move powerfully and with grounded support for their dreams. The Nine offers the

Eight the opportunity to lean into unusual softness and comfort, both initially and as they come back to the Nine for support time and again. The Nine allows the Eight to feel that there is a space for trust in this world after all, which opens up the weary heart of the Eight and allows them to more eagerly offer a powerful path for the Nine to thrive.

Heal: The Eight brings back the often lost voice of the Nine. The Nine often brings the Eight on a quest toward innocence and gentle comfort they often didn't know existed until they met the Nine. Both are secure in knowing their partner, who is a body type like them, also values goodness, justice, and fairness. Their juxtaposition of peace and power allows them to both press forward into goals and relax together well.

Shadows and Throwing Shade: The Eight-Nine pairing can have huge issues when they aren't aligned on core values or preferences. This can occur during intense work or child-rearing seasons. Compromise will be in order, but both can be stubborn. The Eight reacts aggressively and the Nine passive-aggressively, so they must work on pausing to consider one another's perspectives. In the same vein, if the Nine does not confront conflicts, the Eight will mistake their stubbornness for weakness and disrespect them. The Nine feels the Eight is tyrannical and controlling, which may be true in times of stress. Both will feel betrayed, and the Nine may run while the Eight seeks vengeance.

Immerse: The Eight and Nine typically process life's issues through the five senses first. Sometimes they read the world differently, so becoming less rigid and more open to other perspectives is key. As they attempt to let go of control, they must learn relaxation as well as continue the fun date nights and vacations that are a necessary secure base for them. They must also learn to self-soothe.

Glow 2.0: As the Eight and Nine emerge from immersing in their work, they are learning to continually discharge all their felt body experiences and instincts. This includes routes for allowing their anger out safely, which often involves intense daily fitness for each. They are direct, they solve issues fast and simply, and they are passionate about having fun. They do need a weekly relationship meeting so they can plan together as fairly as possible and so the family team can win instead of just one of them.

Afterglow: An Eight and Nine pair takes on missions to help bring justice to the world, whether through employer-employee relations or passionate causes such as the environment, children, the elderly, or animals. When they're intentional and schedule week by week, they can empower one another's big dreams with physical energy and space as they rest. Doing fun fitness together, finding favorite comfort shows, allowing physical activities to discharge their energy, and sharing deep conversations together all become possible as they continue to speak about their issues.

Type Nine with a Type Nine

Shine: Two Nines shine out together with playfulness, wit, adoration, and a fun style of loving that exudes comfort. As both like to keep a positive, harmonious mindset, they try to honor one another's pleasures. They help one another to feel content and safe in the physical environment and with the five senses. This is a pleasure they can collectively indulge in as a twin pairing. Though they have nuances, there is an inner knowing of shared typology and lovely common experiences and rhythms, which they can come back to after hard work for shared comfortability time and again.

Heal: Two Nines affirm one another's backstory of not being heard or validated. Having a partner to remind them of their value in the world is a majorly healing gift. This validation can help their gifts to glow brightly through the entire relationship if they're intentional to empower each other's voices. Peacefully and purposefully boosting one another are excellent ways that each spouse can validate the woundedness of the other and heal them across time and seasons.

Shadows and Throwing Shade: As caring as Nines are about one another theoretically, often they don't find the time to care for themselves or each other, so anger goes undigested in their bodies. Thus, one or both can feel self-righteous, angry, and victimized. Sometimes it's just easier to skip into a tired oblivion and to check out of partner and self-care. It's important for Nines to hear one another and to make an effort even when they're tired or they want to only stay positive. However, withdrawing into themselves will only deepen the shadows and block true intimacy and the shared holding of rich experiences, both hard and good.

Immerse: Nines do well to begin with bodywork individually, even if the other partner is not willing to. This will help with discharging some of their pent-up anger. Next is remembering that conflicts need to be addressed for a relationship. Speaking with energy and directness about those conflicts will help them thrive. They can still be strong, loving, and diplomatic as they embrace their peacefulness and mediation skills for compromise. Though they may feel like being direct temporarily created the dreaded disharmony, the gifts of truth, healing, and connection will surpass these fears as their spouse is drawn to their love, power, and magnetism.

Glow 2.0: Two Nines are extremely strong, capable, and often quite witty and fun as they connect on a grounded, present, and direct level with one another. They know how to give and how to rest. They make prioritized lists, embrace fitness, and make healthy

266

choices together across seasons but also know how to indulge and have fun for a few hours each day. They schedule in times for discussing stressful topics weekly or monthly, perhaps even adding in a fun element like enjoying snacks or watching a favorite show together afterward.

Afterglow: Nines together can enjoy fun dates and daily time, with their often-grounded sense of humor, the sheer comfort they exude, and the good convictions they bring to the world they bless. Two Nines who are awake and vibrant are absolutely unstoppable in both their quest for and their execution of love and justice.

A Call to Cast Your Unique Light Together

Although all couples have shadows and seasons of burnout, when the shadows do find you, you now have the tools for reigniting your love as you immerse in the good work of relationship care time and again.

Do not give up on your quest to shed light on your collective shadows. It will require deep breaths, pauses, sacrifices for one another, and finding healthy rhythms of rest. Thankfully, the Enneagram gives much nuance for doing this work with precision. As we are reminded in Hebrews 10:24, "Let us consider *how* we may spur one another on toward love and good deeds" (emphasis added).

Loving our partner well may not always feel easy in the moment, but as C. S. Lewis's wife, Joy Davidman Lewis, recalls in *Letters to an American Lady*, encouraging or serving others with our unique gifts is a privilege, one we do not always get to carry to the end of our lives.[4] As she candidly shares about the loss of mobility that occurred in her dying days, we are reminded that we will deeply miss being useful when we are no longer able to serve.

Yet even knowing this, you will err at times, so if and when you're driving down a dark road once again, remember the tools you learned here to light the path. There is grace and even redemption on the often shadowy road of walking toward virtue and refinement. Issues aside, we are valuable. Broken people and places are still beloved. As Wendell Berry said, "There are no unsacred places; there are only sacred places and desecrated places."[5]

I believe that even along with the stopping points where mistakes are made and rest is needed, you will walk with courage, resolve, compassion, and gratitude again and again as you seek to bring light to your marriage. You will ignite your bright, colorful glow together in a world of shadows. This is your sacred mission as a couple—casting your unique love and light into these dark or desecrated spaces in yourselves, in each other, and in the world.

> You are the light of the world. A town built on a hill cannot be hidden. Neither do people light a lamp and put it under a bowl. Instead they put it on its stand, and it gives light to everyone in the house. (Matt. 5:14–15)

Glossary

aggressive-assertive stance. The tendency for Threes, Sevens, and Eights to assert themselves actively or independently toward others when they are experiencing stress in most social situations.

attachment wound. When a person's spouse or other main attachment figure hurts them deeply, causing an emotional severing in the bond, which then requires healing for healthy attachment to resume.

attunement. Tuning in to a partner's bodily, mental, and emotional cues with one's own body, mind, and emotions. This does not mean the person feels the same way but that they are compassionately tuned in.

availability bias. A typical pattern of humans to rely on what immediately comes to mind rather than processing what may be going on with intention and fuller reasoning.

bodywork. A process of allowing one's body to wake up to need and to receive care and the working out of stress through fitness, meditation, breathwork, massage, or other bodily stress outlets.

compliant-dependent stance. The tendency for Ones, Twos, and Sixes to be culturally agreeable and move toward others when they are experiencing stress in most social situations.

doing-inhibited. The stance of types Four, Five, and Nine, who often exhibit a repressed doing/action orientation due to melancholy (Fours), scarcity (Fives), or sloth (Nines).

EFT therapist. A clinician trained in emotionally focused therapy, a family systems treatment style developed by Sue Johnson that utilizes attachment and bonding repair in the treatment of a couple's issues. (Visit www.iceeft.com to locate an EFT therapist.)

emotional flooding. An experience of feeling overwhelmed in some capacity and not knowing how to handle it. Depending on their Enneagram orientation, a person may use a fight, flight, freeze, or fawn response to reduce overwhelm.

emotional scanning. The usually unconscious process of scanning for emotional cues from a partner or others a person engages with in bonding processes.

Enneagram Glow. A relationship overlay across time as a couple walks through various relationship stages together.

essence. The inherent best of each type—in other words, the healthiest mental and emotional display of a person.

family systems therapy. A branch of therapy that sees couples and families as core parts of an interworking network, where each person plays an integral role in individual, family, and community wellness.

feeling-inhibited. The stance of types Three, Seven, and Eight, who often exhibit a repressed feeling/emotional orientation due to an excess of doing (Threes), kinetic movement (Sevens), or dominance (Eights).

fundamental attribution error. A common human experience in which a person evaluates another's (e.g., a marriage partner's) motivations or behaviors based on their less appealing personality traits while the person's own motivations and behaviors are given more self-compassion.

future orientation. The tendency for Threes, Sevens, and Eights to look ahead to the future more than to the past or present, rather than trying to balance all three time orientations.

independent stance. See *aggressive-assertive stance.*

instinctual sequence. The order in which a person's instincts for survival kick in. For example, they may rely first on social instincts, then self-preservation instincts, and finally sexual or one-to-one instincts.

neuroplasticity. The ability of the brain to continually modify and adapt its structure and function throughout life and in response to experience.

past orientation. The tendency of Fours, Fives, and Nines to look back at the past more than at the present or the future, rather than trying to balance all three time orientations.

present orientation. The tendency of Ones, Twos, and Sixes to look at the present more than to the future or past, rather than trying to balance all three time orientations.

pursuer-distancer cycle. The tendency of couples to fall into an attachment pattern of one partner pursuing rather aggressively and the other partner retreating into a withdrawing stance, versus them having a stance of balance and interplay.

reaction formation. A defense strategy used to cope with stress, in which a person pretends to be happy with something they are actively upset about but that they do not feel permission to express due to low self-worth or anxiety of some sort.

shadow living. Living out the underbelly of personality, ego, and instincts, without intentional activation of balance or reform.

shadow/shadow side. A term derived from Jungian concepts for the parts of oneself that are less balanced and healthy. These parts may be dismissed by or unconsciously hidden from oneself but are often obvious to their partner or family, inhibiting their growth together.

spiritual release. A practice or experience of allowing one's life stresses to be released to God and to God's plans after one has done their part.

stance. How a person behaves in response to others in terms of repressed centers of intelligence (feeling, thinking, or doing). For a fuller synopsis of stances, see Suzanne Stabile's book *The Journey Toward Wholeness: Enneagram Wisdom for Stress, Balance, and Transformation.*

stimming. A repetitive coping pattern of physical movements that may be part of a person's internal process for emotional regulation and self-soothing.

thinking-inhibited. The stance of types One, Two, and Six, who often represent a repressed or blocked critical thinking/ mental orientation due to an excess of self-criticism (Ones), emotional overuse (Twos), or worry (Six).

time orientation. The centering of attention on various time patterns—past focused (Four, Five, Nine), present focused (One, Two, Six), or future focused (Three, Seven, Eight). This is discussed more fully as it relates to the stances in Suzanne Stabile's book *The Journey Toward Wholeness*.

withdrawing stance. The tendency for Fours, Fives, and Nines to withdraw and move away from others when they are experiencing stress in many social situations.

Acknowledgments

The Enneagram in Marriage is truly an expression of a collective process. I cannot thank the following people enough for helping to create it.

I greatly thank all the individuals and couples who have shared their hearts and souls with me as friends, in sessions, or in the Enneagram and Marriage community. Your journey is sacred and beautiful, something I hold with the deepest respect and love. I am always inspired to keep pressing on in faith as we fulfill our lives' callings together.

I thank my husband, Wes, for pursuing me even before I knew our destiny together. I'm amazed and continually humbled to see the ways we've carried one another across decades and to see the many lives we impact when we risk bringing our gifts and glow together. Thank you for loving me just as I am and also balancing me with your vision of who we can be. We are truly better together.

To my children, Hannah, Melody, and Jack. You are the greatest gifts I'll ever get to hold for a little while, and I treasure each second together. I love seeing your gifts emerge and your beautiful "sibling glow" as well. I hope that one day you find encouragement for your own adult relationships through the lessons learned in these pages.

A huge thanks to the team at Baker Books: Rachel O'Connor, Wendy Wetzel, Laura Powell, the exquisite Jessica English, Hannah Boers, Sarah Traill, Carrie Krause, and especially my editor Stephanie Duncan Smith. Your words and encouragement—strong and passionate but soothing—have helped me to be a braver writer than I ever dared to be. Your gentle yet challenging insights called me to an authenticity and depth I could not foresee, and I'm forever grateful.

I have so much love for Ariel Curry Editorial—for Ariel's thoughtfulness and encouragement to bring this piece to publication and for pointing me to the Christopher Ferebee Agency.

To Christopher Ferebee and the team at the Christopher Ferebee Agency. I can't thank you enough for working diligently to bring this project to light in a more beautiful, dignified, and clarified way and for helping me to find such a perfect fit in Stephanie and the Baker team.

To my siblings, Holly, David, and Abbie, and my in-laws, the Hardin family. I thank you for the great and deep love—seen and unseen—that you continue to share with our family, and for your encouragement and examples of sacrificial love across many seasons.

To my team of therapists and coaches: Lori Odendahl-Klemish, LMHC; Glenda Reagan, LMHC; Melissa Thompson; and Jenn Johnson (and our honorary board members Craig Stratton and Chris Reagan). I could not have even begun this book in good conscience without knowing that you would be working so hard to love on our local community at Reflections Counseling, and I thank you greatly for reflecting the love of Christ to those you serve.

To Jenn Johnson, my executive assistant, and her husband, Robb. Thank you for responding to the call when you felt led to reach out to me and for holding out faith with me for the things we did not yet see with this book and this process. Here it is!

To my E + M inner circle of coaches, I greatly thank you as well. You were the earliest initiators of E + M, and I love knowing we came together so majestically. I especially thank the deep divers—Alicia Larkey, Christine Willeford, Melissa Thompson, Kirsten Barker, and Krista McNally—for the gift of fire and encouragement when I needed it most!

Thank you to Wes Hardin, artist Alaina Pompa, and marriage therapist Michael Shahan, LMFT, for being early theoretical contributors of the glow between a couple.

Thank you to Julie Relyea for her help with this book as my citation research assistant. Your organization and detail helped to bring such peace and precision to this work, and I can't thank you enough.

Thank you to Shyla Rose Photography for finding the light in your beautiful photography for this book.

Thank you, Carla Hulslander, for being an insightful friend and for inhabiting your Four space so well when you challenged me to take a deeper dive into the Enneagram.

Thank you to Hannah Hardin for your clarifying interior illustrations.

Thank you to my dearest friends, Stacey Day, Amy Crowe, Anna Herzog, AnnMarie Jones, Renee LaBelle, Becka Eggleston, and Rachel Porta; our dearest couple friends-like-family, the Taylors, the Kittredges, the Partons, the Crowes, the McKinleys, and the Grays; and the many others who have prayed for us, held us up in faith and standards of integrity, and otherwise helped us to make this marriage and book possible. Let's shine out for Christ continually.

Olivia and Bridget, thank you for being prayer warriors along the way from the book's beginnings and for the earliest podcast encouragements.

Finally, I forever remain grateful for the first marriage I ever saw, my late parents Don and Nancy Masse's very *The Notebook* relationship. Their love across seasons for one another has been an enduring model of sacrifice and tenacity through both good times and hard times on the journey, and I will never forget their many sacrifices for me.

My greatest gratitude will always go to God for the outpouring of Christ's love, for renewal of energy each day, for quiet and deeply personal blessings, and most of all, for the joy of the Lord that is my deepest and most enduring strength.

Notes

Introduction

1. Thomas Aquinas, *Summa Theologica* (Claremont, CA: Coyote Canyon Press, 2010), loc. 5139 of 6640, Kindle.

2. Carl Gustav Jung, *Modern Man in Search of a Soul*, trans. W. S. Dell and Cary Baynes (Christopher Prince, 2011), loc. 49 of 251, Kindle.

3. Ian Morgan Cron and Suzanne Stabile, *The Road Back to You: An Enneagram Journey to Self-Discovery* (Downers Grove, IL: InterVarsity Press, 2016).

4. Beatrice Chestnut, *The Complete Enneagram: 27 Paths to Greater Self-Knowledge* (Berkeley: She Writes Press, 2013), 43.

5. Chestnut, *Complete Enneagram*, 51.

6. "Four Temperament," ScienceDirect, accessed January 10, 2023, https://www.sciencedirect.com/topics/psychology/four-temperament.

7. "Enneagram Typing: Family and Culture Overlays," The Enneagram in Business, April 9, 2018, https://theenneagraminbusiness.com/typing/enneagram-typing-family-and-culture-overlays.

Chapter 1 The Stages of Your Enneagram Glow across Time

1. J. R. R. Tolkien, *The Lord of the Rings: The Two Towers* (New York: Mariner Books, 2002), loc. 631 of 1179, Kindle.

2. Robert Frost, "Nothing Gold Can Stay," in *The Poetry of Robert Frost: The Collected Poems*, ed. Edward Lathem (New York: Henry Holt and Company, 1962).

3. J. R. R. Tolkien, *The Lord of the Rings: The Fellowship of the Ring* (New York: Mariner Books, 2002), loc. 169 of 1179, Kindle.

4. Jane Austen, *Persuasion*, in *The Complete Novels of Jane Austen* (San Diego, CA: Canterbury Classics, 2019), 1107.

5. Darkness is a phase some couples experience between shadows and immersion, and it is the absence of hope. This is where you may have picked up this book or decided to visit a coach or counselor. Some face divorce here, as you may have experienced. There is no judgment if this is part of your journey, and I'm glad you're learning with me. If you're in this stage, I highly recommend working with a trained professional.

Chapter 2 The Enneagram and Levels of Relationship Health in Marriage

1. Jane Austen, *Pride and Prejudice*, in *The Complete Novels of Jane Austen*, 318.
2. Cron and Stabile, *Road Back to You*, 90.
3. Jane Austen, *Sense and Sensibility*, in *The Complete Novels of Jane Austen*, 49.

Chapter 3 Learning to Love One Another with Head, Heart, Body, and Soul

1. Wendell Berry, "A Jonquil for Mary Penn," in *Fidelity: Five Stories* (Berkeley: Counterpoint, 2018), loc. 80 of 190, Kindle.
2. John M. Gottman and Nan Silver, *The Seven Principles for Making Marriage Work* (New York: Harmony Books, 2015), loc. 16 of 298, Kindle.
3. Oxford Learner's Dictionaries, s.v. "synergy," accessed June 6, 2022, https://www.oxfordlearnersdictionaries.com/us/definition/english/synergy?q=synergy.
4. Suzanne Stabile, *The Journey Toward Wholeness: Enneagram Wisdom for Stress, Balance, and Transformation* (Downers Grove, IL: InterVarsity Press, 2021), 18–21.
5. John Mark Comer, *The Ruthless Elimination of Hurry* (Colorado Springs: Waterbrook, 2019), 57.
6. Hillary McBride, *The Wisdom of Your Body: Finding Healing, Wholeness, and Connection through Embodied Living* (Grand Rapids: Brazos, 2021), loc. 22 of 280, Kindle.

Chapter 4 Fighting for Your Survival

1. Gregory Alan Isakov, "Second Chances," accessed January 17, 2023, https://gregoryalanisakov.com/songs/second-chances.
2. Carrie Cokely, "Rosie the Riveter," *Britannica*, accessed June 6, 2022, https://www.britannica.com/topic/Rosie-the-Riveter.
3. Lin-Manuel Miranda and Opetaia Tavita Foa'i, "We Know the Way," track 5 on *Moana: Original Motion Picture Soundtrack*, Walt Disney, 2016.
4. Aulii Cravalho and Rachel House, "I Am Moana (Song of the Ancestors)," track 10 on *Moana: Original Motion Picture Soundtrack*, Walt Disney, 2016.
5. "The Three Instincts: Our Animal Drives," Chestnut Paes Enneagram Academy, accessed June 6, 2022, https://cpenneagram.com/instincts.
6. Bea Chestnut, "Instincts in Marriage with Bea Chestnut," March 7, 2022, in *Enneagram and Marriage*, produced by Christa Hardin, podcast, https://pod

casts.apple.com/us/podcast/instincts-in-marriage-with-beatrice-chestnut/id
1493137938?i=1000553149087.

7. Chestnut, *Complete Enneagram*, 16.

8. "Marriage and Couples," The Gottman Institute, accessed June 6, 2022, https://www.gottman.com/about/research/couples/.

9. Zach Brittle, "Manage Conflict—Part 4," The Gottman Institute, accessed June 23, 2022, https://www.gottman.com/blog/manage-conflict-part-4/#:
~:text=The%20fact%20that%20your%20heart,relationship%20setting%2C
%20that%27s%20called%20flooding.

10. Aundi Kolber, *Try Softer* (Carol Stream, IL: Tyndale, 2020).

Chapter 5 Throwing Shade

1. Sue Johnson, *Hold Me Tight: Seven Conversations for a Lifetime of Love* (New York: Little, Brown and Co., 2008), loc. 174 of 267, Kindle.

2. "Fundamental Attribution Error and How It's Destroying Your Relationships," Professional Leadership Institute, accessed June 9, 2022, https://profes
sionalleadershipinstitute.com/personality/fundamental-attribution-error-and
-how-its-eroding-your-relationships.

3. McBride, *Wisdom of Your Body*, loc. 247 of 280, Kindle.

Chapter 6 Soul Care and Marriage

1. Charlotte Brontë, *Jane Eyre* (New York: Signet Classics, 1997), 320.

2. David N. Daniels and Suzanne Dion, *The Enneagram, Relationships, and Intimacy: Understanding One Another Leads to Loving Better and Living More Fully* (self-pub., 2018), loc. 54 and 62–66 of 536, Kindle.

Chapter 7 Glow 2.0

1. Tolkien, *Fellowship of the Ring*, loc. 247 of 1197, Kindle.

2. John Gottman, "John Gottman on Trust and Betrayal," *Greater Good Magazine*, October 29, 2011, https://greatergood.berkeley.edu/article/item/john_gott
man_on_trust_and_betrayal.

3. Tolkien, *Fellowship of the Ring*, loc. 348 of 1197, Kindle.

4. Curt Thompson, *Anatomy of the Soul: Surprising Connections between Neuroscience and Spiritual Practices That Can Transform Your Life and Relationships* (Carol Stream, IL: SaltRiver, 2010), 107–8.

Chapter 8 Afterglow

1. Charlotte Brontë, *Jane Eyre* (Floyd, VA: Wilder Publications, 2014), loc. 388 of 696, Kindle.

2. John Gottman and Joan DeClaire, *The Relationship Cure: A 5 Step Guide to Strengthening Your Marriage, Family, and Friendships* (New York: Three Rivers, 2002), loc. 41 of 309, Kindle.

3. Penny Marshall, dir., *A League of Their Own* (Hollywood, CA: Parkway Productions, 1992).

4. J. R. R. Tolkien, *The Hobbit* (New York: Del Ray, 2020), 235.

The Glow Pairing Dictionary

1. Brontë, *Jane Eyre*, loc. 482 of 696, Kindle.

2. Taylor Swift, "Illicit Affairs," track 10 on *Folklore*, epublic Records, 2020.

3. J. R. R. Tolkien, *Two Towers*, loc. 376 of 1179, Kindle.

4. C. S. Lewis, *Letters to an American Lady* (Grand Rapids: Eerdmans, 1967), 73.

5. Wendell Berry, *Given* (Berkeley, CA: Counterpoint Press, 2006), loc. 24 of 133, Kindle.

CHRISTA HARDIN

has been counseling and coaching couples for over two decades, and she holds a master's in clinical psychology from Wheaton College. Christa hosts the popular podcast *Enneagram and Marriage*, an outreach dedicated to fueling couples by linking the best of relationship research and personality study, and it has surpassed over one million downloads. Christa ardently loves all things Middle-earth and Jane Austen, and she and her husband, Wes, live in a South Florida "shire" with their three children, Hannah, Melody, and Jack.

CONNECT WITH CHRISTA

EnneagramInYourMarriage.com

f @Enneagram&Marriage

@EnneagramAndMarriage